Vegetarian Cooking Without

Note to the Reader

The recipes and information in this book are not meant to be prescriptive. Any attempt to treat a medical condition should always come under the direction of a competent physician. Neither the publishers nor the author can accept responsibility for illness arising from a failure by a reader to take medical advice.

Vegetarian Cooking Without

Recipes free from added gluten, sugar, dairy products, yeast, salt and saturated fat

BARBARA COUSINS

Some information may be out of date as medical research progresses and may not be applicable to all patients.

PLEASE CONSULT YOUR DOCTOR

Thorsons

Thorsons
An Imprint of HarperCollins*Publishers*
77–85 Fulham Palace Road
Hammersmith, London W6 8JB

The Thorsons website address is: www.thorsons.com

Published by Thorsons 2000

3 5 7 9 10 8 6 4

A catalogue record for this book
is available from the British Library

ISBN 0 7225 3897 9

Printed in Great Britain by
Martins the Printers Ltd, Berwick-upon-Tweed

Contents

Introduction

Following the success of my first volume of *Cooking Without*, I was asked to write a follow-up. I decided that this time I would write a vegetarian version, mainly because good vegetarian recipes are harder to find when avoiding the use of cream, cheese, wheat etc. I know that many individuals who enjoyed the recipes in my first book have been requesting more, so here they are. I must admit that I quite impress myself at times when I create wonderful new dishes without the use of so many foods that seem essential ingredients in many people's diets. It just goes to show that eating can be a pleasure even for those on restricted regimes.

Although I have written a little about the reasons for cooking without certain foods, I didn't want to make this text a repeat of my first book because there is so much more I want to say. Being in practice as a nutritional therapist I am continually learning new information and I would like to impart some of this information to you. I have had lots of feedback about the introductory section in *Cooking Without* and the consensus of opinion seems to be that it is a simple and common sense approach to health and healing. I would like this volume to continue that approach in some new areas of understanding.

Food is a serious business. We are what we eat and food is our fuel. Yet, it is only in the last few years that food has finally begun to be recognised in the West as being an important aspect of health and healing. Naturopaths and nutritional therapists have always been aware of the effect of diet, not only on our physical health but also on our mental and emotional wellbeing. There has, however, been a reluctance by many people to accept this. Diet is the foundation of our health, we cannot abuse our bodies by feeding it a poor diet and then expect therapists or doctors to be able to make us better.

Since the advent of modern agriculture and food processing techniques, our diet has moved further and further away from the natural foods which have sustained traditional communities all over the world for centuries. Individuals in such communities live on a mainly vegetarian diet of whole grains, beans, locally grown vegetables and fruits with small quantities of meat and fish eaten when available. Nowadays meat, sugar and fat consumption has generally taken over from traditional diets and the consumption of vegetables, fruit, grains and pulses has substantially declined. Added to this is the fact that most of the food on supermarket shelves bears little or no resemblance to its origins. It has been over-processed, coloured, flavoured, textured, preserved, packaged, flown half way round the world and will probably keep for years. Good food goes off. The trick is to eat it before it does.

A healthy eating lifestyle starts with recognising that symptoms of illness don't just happen – they are the body's way of letting us know that all is not well and we have had a hand in creating the problem. Illness represents an invitation to change to a healthier way of living which will not only renew our physical bodies but will calm the mind and the emotions as well.

It really is wonderful at last to see so many people taking responsibility for their own, and their family's, health. For too long there has been a mystical 'they'. 'They' wouldn't let us eat food that was harmful. 'They' should provide us with the drugs or operations to heal us. Unfortunately, 'they' are often more concerned with their profits, or their power, rather than with our health.

Vegetarianism and Detoxification

Research shows that eating a vegetarian diet improves one's chance of avoiding many serious health problems, but that is only the case if you eat a wholesome vegetarian diet. I remember once employing two workmen one of whom told me he was a vegetarian. At lunchtime they disappeared and I saw them sitting outside in their van eating lunch. As it was a miserable cold day, I went outside to invite them in. The vegetarian was eating chips with white bread, the non-vegetarian was tucking into a tuna rice salad with wholemeal bread which he had prepared that morning!

Eating a wholesome vegetarian diet encourages toxicity to be removed from the body. If you study the diagram below you will see meat, fish, eggs etc, at one end of a sliding scale, while fruit and salads and vegetables are at the other end. Those foods on the left side of the scale help to keep toxicity in the body and will even be craved to push toxicity back in if it comes out too quickly. At the other end of the scale are, first of all, the fruits. Fruits pull toxicity out of the cells, though not necessarily out of the body. In the past, fruit fasts were recommended by naturopaths as a therapy to cure ill health. Nowadays, however, most people's bodies, and in particular their livers (the main organ of detoxification), are too suppressed to cope with the sudden surge of toxicity which comes out of the cells when eating lots of fruit and fruit juices. This means that individuals these days often feel too ill on a fruit fast to be able to continue. Raw vegetables and salads are the next most eliminative foods, followed by cooked vegetables, which still eliminate but in a less aggressive way than fruit or even salads. Leafy green vegetables are stronger eliminators than root vegetables.

In the middle of the sliding scale are the grains and it is here where we find a balance between the amount of toxicity pulled out of the cells and that eliminated to the outside world. Grains, such as rice, millet, quinoa and buckwheat, are superb at soaking up toxicity and helping to

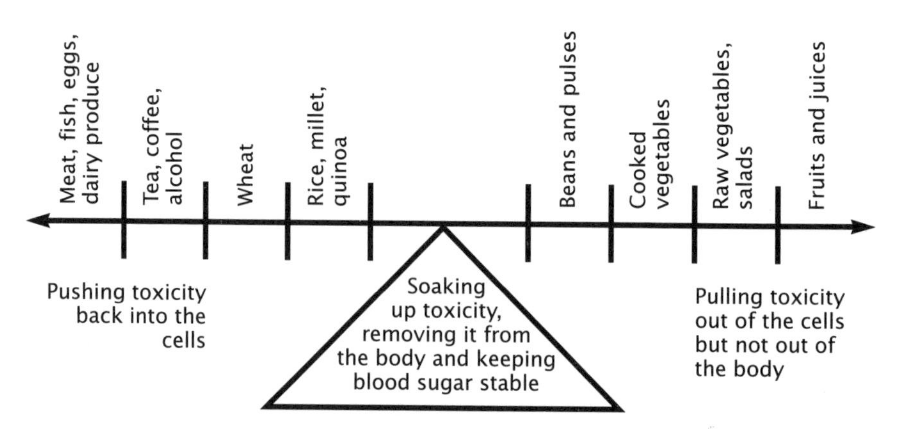

Balancing the elimination of toxicity

remove it from the body. They are also excellent at supporting the blood sugar in order that the body has sufficient energy to remove the toxicity. The art of staying healthy is to find our own individual balance along the sliding scale. Generally this means eating lots of foods from the middle section, such as grains, pulses, beans and vegetables, with foods from either end being added in more limited quantities to add interest and flavour to our diet. This fine balance of health is a little like a see-saw and it is important to listen to our bodies on a daily basis in order to discover how to adjust our diets in order to maintain this balance. Too little of the right food and we stay where we are, entrenched in our illness and emotional pain; too much detoxification and we eliminate toxicity too quickly causing us more illness and emotional pain.

Pulling too much toxicity out of the cells but not out of the body is one reason why individuals often feel ill when starting a healthy eating regime. The same effect can occur when introducing minerals in supplement form, as these also encourage toxicity to move out of the cells. I always suggest that anyone changing their diet does so gradually and that supplements are also introduced gradually. In this way one obtains balance and can feel quite well while removing toxicity from the body. There is no benefit to be gained by trying to speed things up, as our livers determine how fast we can detoxify. Unfortunately, today, many people's livers are so overworked dealing with the toxicity in food and the atmosphere, not to mention high-fat diets, unexpressed emotions, suppression from drugs and alcohol etc., that they have to be encouraged to eliminate toxicity. If we try to go faster than the liver can manage, then the toxicity backs up in the blood stream making the individual feel poorly. It can lead to an exacerbation of original symptoms or new symptoms can appear such as headaches, aching limbs, tiredness, stomach upsets or even mental and emotional symptoms such as anger or depression. Sometimes, the body will catch an infection to try to throw off the excess toxicity to the outside world.

Pulling too much toxicity out of the cells can also encourage cravings for certain foods; usually the suppressive ones in the left-hand column of the sliding scale diagram above. Sometimes, individuals have great difficulty giving up such foods as wheat, meat, tea or coffee because toxicity floods out of their cells into their system too quickly and they end up back on these foods to arrest its flow. Other people manage to eat lots of fruit and raw salads and cope well with the amount of toxicity eliminated into their systems. The idea of a sliding scale is that each person finds their balance. This balance may vary from day to day and will depend on our energy levels. There is a maximum amount of energy we can produce each day and this energy is dependent on keeping the blood sugar stable by eating sufficient of the right kind of food at regular intervals. If, however, we then use this energy to rush around, overwork or worry then the energy will not be available to remove toxicity from our bodies. Listening to how our body feels is the only way to find this balance. If we are having a good day and feeling great then our body will cope with extra fruit or salads. If we are having a bad day and can feel a backlog of toxicity in the body then it is a day for eating lots of grains to soak up the excess. Learn to listen to your body and adjust your diet accordingly.

Being a vegetarian isn't right for everyone (see Yin and Yang on page 17) but it does encourage detoxification and many individuals would see tremendous health improvements by reducing or cutting out animal proteins.

Blood sugar balance

I talk extensively about blood sugar in my first *Cooking Without* book, but I want to mention it here because I feel that raising the blood sugar is the most important thing we do on the path to good health. Blood sugar is about energy and with insufficient energy the body cannot detoxify and heal. Energy is needed not only for us to complete our everyday tasks, but also for those internal organs which have jobs to do to keep our bodies running smoothly. Blood sugar is also needed for the brain. Insufficient blood sugar to the brain means we get symptoms such as headaches, muzzy heads, poor concentration, anxiety and depression.

The following chart shows a day in the life of your blood sugar. Whenever I show this chart to groups and ask if there is anyone who doesn't have a blood sugar problem the answer is always negative. In fact, in 14 years in practice as a nutritional therapist, I have not met a patient who did not have a blood sugar problem. Blood sugar problems underlie all health problems. Hopefully no one will have all the symptoms listed below but anyone experiencing some of these has room for health improvements.

A day in the life of your blood sugar

MORNING
Difficulty getting going – need tea, coffee or a cigarette to start the day
Wake with a muzzy head or headache
Feel sick or nauseous first thing
Not hungry for breakfast
Feel negative or depressed first thing
Feel bad all day after a lie in
Feel hungrier for breakfast after a large, late evening meal

MID-MORNING
Cravings for tea, coffee, cigarettes, biscuits, toast etc.
Difficulty concentrating
Feeling tired
Headache or muzzy head

LUNCHTIME
Feel tired after eating lunch
Shaky, trembly or dizzy if lunch is missed

MID-AFTERNOON
Mood changes – feeling negative, can't be bothered, irritable or depressed
Feel tired, yawning
Headache or muzzy head
Difficulty concentrating, forgetful
Better with deadlines to meet

EVENING
Snacking while preparing food
Don't feel full after evening meal
Need something sweet to end the evening meal
Tired after eating

Fall asleep when sitting down
Wanting to nibble all evening

NIGHT TIME
Panic attacks, palpitations, sweating
Hunger in the middle of the night
Waking in the night with a busy mind

Raising the blood sugar by means of diet involves eating sufficient of the right kind of food at regular intervals. I recommend my patients eat six times per day. (*Cooking Without* has suggested eating regimes). By raising the blood sugar, the body not only obtains sufficient energy to detoxify and heal but low blood sugar symptoms (such as those above) start to disappear and the individual feels good while the body is healing.

Most of my patients feel between 50–90% better within three weeks just by changing their diets. However, that isn't the end of the story, as these people would need to stay with the diet and always eat six times per day in order to stay well. In order that more flexibility can be obtained the answer is to detoxify the body of any physical, mental or emotional toxicity. Obviously, diet goes a long way towards achieving this detoxification but other aids can speed the process, such as raising the mineral status of the body using supplementation, or counselling to help remove emotional toxicity. This is where seeing a qualified therapist is useful, but the foundation of a good detoxifying diet will assist any other therapy to work more successfully.

Raising the blood sugar by means of diet means that pressure is taken off the liver and adrenal glands. The liver is our back-up support as far as blood sugar is concerned. The liver should provide a release of blood sugar if food has not been eaten or if extra energy is needed. However, most people's livers these days are struggling to cope with a backlog of toxicity and are more likely to say 'forget it, I've got too much to do', rather than act as a back-up support. Until the body has been detoxified and its mineral status is good, the liver cannot be expected to provide a good blood sugar releasing service. If the liver is struggling to cope providing a back-up service, and the individual is not eating six times per day, then the only other place the body can get energy from is the adrenal glands.

The adrenal glands provide an emergency supply of blood sugar.

They are there for the 'flight or fight' response. Think of it like the money that one puts in the building society for a rainy day. It won't last long if we keep dipping into it each day. The same applies to the adrenal glands, they soon run out of reserves if we use them each day instead of feeding ourselves properly and obtaining our energy from suitable food. People, however, soon learn ways of kicking the adrenal glands to provide an extra surge of blood sugar. This may sound like a good idea, but eventually the adrenal glands stop responding and we have a permanent state of fatigue. Most individuals these days go round with adrenal glands which are exhausted, and they too, are exhausted. An extreme example of adrenal exhaustion is the condition of Chronic Fatigue (M.E.). Blood pressure can be a good indicator of adrenal exhaustion. It is always low when the adrenal glands are tiring.

Kicking the adrenal glands

Below is a list of the things we use to kick the adrenal glands into action when they are tiring:

Alcohol	Cigarettes
Tea and coffee	Stress
Excitement	Work
Allergens	Sport

Throughout the day stimulants are frequently used to kick the adrenals. Because we go a long time without eating during the night some individuals whose blood sugar has dropped too low overnight will find mornings the worst time of day. They may feel negative or depressed, sickly or headachy or unable to get going without tea, coffee or a cigarette to kick the adrenal glands into action. Others will feel fine when they wake because the adrenal glands are rested, but they will then flag mid-morning or mid-afternoon when the adrenal glands run out of reserves. Interestingly, eating late at night will support the blood sugar so that it is not as low in the mornings. People who frequently don't feel hungry at breakfast time will often notice that they feel hungrier after eating a large meal later than normal on the previous evening.

Allergens can be used to kick the blood sugar. Any food we are allergic to, or intolerant of, is a stress on the body and can cause the adrenal glands to produce energy. This can be seen in hyperactive children, when one glass of orange juice causes them to run around like a whirlwind. With some people, allergens have the opposite effect and cause their blood sugar to drop still further. This is illustrated in the case of my husband and myself, alcohol makes me want to go to sleep while he becomes full of life. We are useless at a party together as I just want to go home and he wants to stay and dance the night away.

Many people use stress or excitement to kick their adrenal glands. Those who need deadlines in order to get work done are leaving things to the last minute in order to get a rush of adrenalin. Workaholics feel better being busy because their adrenalin is flowing, and they will often feel depressed or lacking in energy when they have a day off. Sport and exercise are often used to kick the adrenal glands of individuals who are tired. They feel better after a workout or jog because the adrenalin is flowing. Others who need constant stimulation or excitement have low blood sugar and do not feel good unless they are living on adrenalin. We can see this on a general level where everyone seems to be rushing round trying to find the next high. I feel this is also the case with a lot of teenage crime. The high that the adrenalin rush causes is more important than the car ride or the stolen property. It is a sad reflection on the state of teenage health and especially their blood sugar levels.

As well as avoiding kicking the adrenal glands, it is also necessary to avoid factors which cause the blood sugar to fall. Thus the adrenal glands and liver are spared from the stress of supporting the blood sugar on a daily basis.

Factors which can cause low blood sugar

Eating sugary or over processed foods
Not eating regularly
High toxicity levels
Overwork
Eating insufficient food
Eating foods to which one is sensitive
Stress

Sugar, sugary snacks and processed carbohydrates are often used to give a quick boost to low blood sugar levels. However, quick boosts are dangerous and so the body produces insulin from the pancreas in order to remove sugar from the blood stream and the result is low blood sugar levels again. Eating sugary foods or processed carbohydrates also means that we rob the body. Firstly, the pancreas needs energy and vitamins and minerals to produce insulin so we rob the body of these each time we eat sugary snacks. Secondly, we could put some food into the body, which is full of goodness, rather than the empty calories which sugary snacks contain. *Cooking Without* and *Vegetarian Cooking Without* contain recipes that are ideal – free from sugar and processed foods and high in complex carbohydrates to lift the blood sugar.

Many individuals don't eat sufficient food. When eating the right kind of food at regular intervals one can eat an amazing amount of food without gaining weight. Going too long without eating is a major cause of not only low blood sugar symptoms but also the cravings for the items we use to kick our adrenal glands. People will find it much harder to give up smoking or avoid tea, coffee or sugar unless they lift their blood sugar first. Individuals who feel ill all day after a lie-in have gone too long without eating. Their blood sugar may be so low that it never lifts that day. Feeling tired after meals is often the result of going too long without food, although the cause could be eating unsuitable foods. If the blood sugar is already low before we eat, it will continue to drop still further after we eat, as energy is needed to digest the food. Later, the blood sugar will lift but in the meantime we may not feel full even though we have eaten a big meal, or we may feel unable to finish a meal without a pudding. Alternatively, we may spend the whole evening snacking. Eating insufficient food can cause problems in the middle of the night. It is a long time from the evening meal until breakfast time and many people have blood sugar levels which cannot remain stable for so long. Thus, the adrenal gland will suddenly switch on in the middle of the night producing symptoms such as panic attacks, anxiety, sweating, palpitations, hunger or a busy mind.

High toxicity levels lower the blood sugar. This may be happening on a permanent basis with someone who is very toxic but is very obvious when detoxification takes place too quickly. It is the reason why I always suggest that individuals change gradually to a healthy eating regime and increase mineral supplements over a period of time.

Although stress and overwork can be used to kick the adrenal glands into action, they can also be the cause of low blood sugar levels. There is oly a certain amount of energy we can produce each day and stress and overwork quickly use up these supplies. In fact, stress can cause the blood sugar to plummet even though we may have eaten very well.

Mental and Emotional Detoxification

Most people are starting to realise the link between their physical health and the food which they eat. It's starting to seem like common sense. However, few realise that diet plays such an important part in our mental and emotional wellbeing.

The two main causes of any disease are toxicity and malnutrition. The interaction between these two means that if we have too much toxicity and insufficient right nutrients, then the toxicity stays inside making us ill; but if we raise the level of nutrition then the toxicity can be eliminated resulting in good health.

We have all heard about toxicity in our food, the air we breathe, in our water supply etc. but we don't often hear about emotional toxicity, yet the cells of the body are actively encoded with every emotional and mental issue that has not been resolved in our lives. Different organs hold on to different emotions so the liver is affected by anger, the kidneys by fear. One of the most important factors in staying healthy is to be true to ourselves. But how do we know who we really are? We may have suppressed our natural instincts and emotions and learnt to behave in certain ways in order to get our needs met. Few of us grow up being able to be in touch with our true feelings and knowing how to express these. The emotional toxicity created by suppression then prevents us from reaching our full potential on any level – physical, mental, emotional or spiritual.

Life can be looked at as a choice between following the 'A' road or the 'B' road.

The 'A' road is the path we are meant to be following in life and it leads us back to God, the higher consciousness, the universal mind or whatever you want to call a higher power. The nearer we stay to the 'A' road in life the easier our life will be. We will still have difficulties, challenges, loss of loved ones etc. to deal with as these are necessary in life to help us to grow and learn, but we will be able to cope with them and each one enables us to move on. In order to stay on the 'A' road we need to listen to our intuition, to be in touch with feelings, our inner knowing

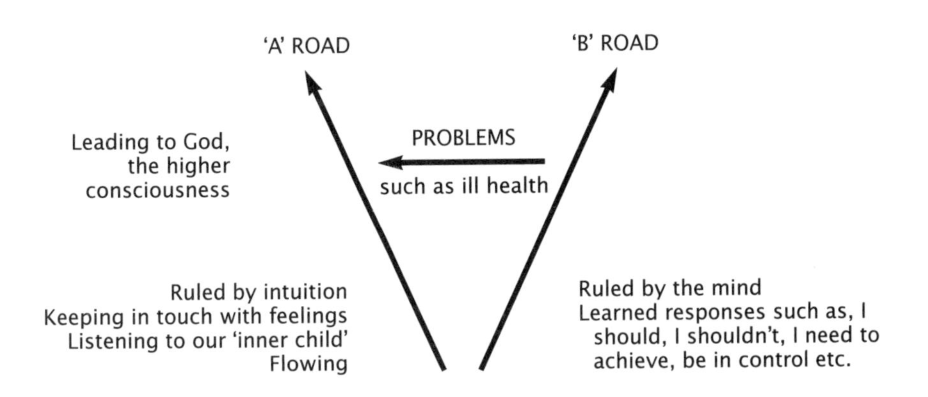

or our 'inner child'. By listening to our intuition we are listening to our higher consciousness and following the path our soul chose before we incarnated on this earth.

However, if we just followed our feeling and intuition without engaging our mind we would soon be in trouble. Our mind tells us not to eat food which is too hot, or to look both ways before crossing the road. The art in life is to balance intuition with the mind, but unfortunately, the western world in which we live encourages the mind to take over. As babies we have strong emotions and feelings which enable us to express our need for food, comfort etc. but we come in with our minds empty. Our minds are gradually filled with what other people want us to know. Our parents, siblings, teachers, society etc. all have a part to play in who we become, irrespective of whether this is in line with our true selves. Often as adults we have lost touch with our feelings and intuition and are ruled by our heads.

Suddenly, we start heading down the 'B' road where our mind takes over, telling us what we should and should not do. Telling us that others will not like us unless we behave in certain ways, telling us we do not deserve to be happy or that we need to achieve in order to feel loved. The list is endless and personal to each individual. The more we have been indoctrinated or abused as children the further down the 'B' road we will be.

When we are heading down the 'B' road our inner guidance will try to communicate with us in alternative ways. The busier we are the harder it will be to hear this guidance which may come through dreams or life experiences. If we still ignore our inner self, then the universe ensures that we encounter problems to encourage us back onto the correct path in life. These problems may be in the area of health or in other areas of life such as work or relationships but, if looked at positively, they can be seen as an invitation to change. It is our higher consciousness saying, 'Will you stop, look and listen? You are heading in the wrong direction'. Problems occur when the body won't let the soul do what it wants to do.

Starting the process of detoxification by eating better quality food means that the body begins to discharge toxicity which has been carried for years, irrespective of whether this has originated from physical, mental or emotional sources. If this toxicity is suppressed with drugs then it will become harder to clear, as it goes deeper into the body. The most important factor for achieving success during detoxification is the willingness to face whatever comes up, learn from it and resolve it by being open to needed changes. The understanding and messages are released as the toxicity moves out of the body.

Eventually, when the body is purified, health is not only obtained on a physical level, but also spontaneity and peace of mind come through being in touch with our spiritual existence and our inner guidance.

The Energetics of foods

For thousands of years China has classified food and disease in relation to energy rather than nutrients and toxicity. Not only does food give us life force or energy, but food is also capable of heating or cooling, drying or moistening, calming the mind or giving us will power.

In Chinese medicine, a practitioner is not interested so much in the disease label, but whether the symptoms are showing that the individual is, for instance, too hot, cold, damp or dry. Oriental traditions do not understand the western view of Candida. We tend to think of being invaded by a micro-organism which must be killed to re-instate health. The Chinese would just say that the person is too damp. Too hot and damp if symptoms such as thrush and cystitis are present; too cold and damp if digestion and bowel problems are present. This idea of not giving the disease power by labelling it feels comfortable for me as I've always felt that the important step in treating Candida was to make the environment one where Candida didn't want to reside.

In practice, I am finding the energetics of food and disease a very helpful way of approaching problems. For instance, our digestion is dependent on sufficient heat, it is like a fire burning fuel. Too much cold, damp fuel and the fire does not burn well. Similarly, too much cold, damp food and we do not digest well. Undigested food residues then travel too far down the digestive tract feeding Candida, which is present in everyone. This helps to explain why people with Candida problems can eat a certain food on one occasion and be fine, yet another day it causes them problems. It all depends on how well their digestion is coping. Sometimes the digestion is affected by a lack of energy as well as cold and moisture. Digestion may be fine early in the day when the energy is good, but it may not cope so well towards the end of the day when it is tiring.

It is interesting to note how patients interpret the diets I give them. All my patients are encouraged to eat lots of vegetables and grains, especially rice. However, some individuals will eat lots of warming meals by choosing foods with a warm energy as well as eating hot meals. They will make lots of curries and casseroles using garlic, ginger and warming spices. Others will be eating their food cold and also choosing foods which have a cold energy, such as salads and fruit with their rice. Often, it is necessary to adjust the way people interpret their diets in order to alleviate symptoms.

People suffering from heat-related symptoms, such as thrush, cystitis, spots, boils, inflammations, hot flushes or dry stools, need to eat more cooling foods. This means eating more foods with a cooling energy, as well as foods which are cool in temperature. Foods recommended for removing heat include alfalfa sprouts, apples, aubergines (eggplant), avocados, barley, beansprouts, broccoli, cauliflower, celery, courgettes (zucchini), cucumber, camomile, lemon, lettuce, millet, mint, melon, marjoram, nettle, orange, peppermint, pineapple, pear, seaweed, spinach, tomato, tofu, tea and wheat.

Individuals suffering from cold-related symptoms, such as poor digestion, bloating, loose stools, alternating constipation and diarrhoea, cold extremities, poor circulation, fatigue and muscle weakness, need to eat food with a warmer temperature and a warmer food energy. Foods with a warming energy include basil, bayleaf, black pepper, caraway, carob, cherry, chestnut, coriander, cinnamon, clove, chilli, cumin, dates, dill seed, fennel, garlic, ginger, horseradish, leek, mustard, nutmeg, onions, oats, oregano, parsnip, peach, quinoa, rosemary, sweet potato, thyme and walnut.

Dampness is a condition which causes many individuals to have health problems, some of which are not visible. Noticeable signs of dampness may include Candida problems, oily skin or hair, sticky perspiration, water retention, a bloated abdomen, discharges, heaviness of the head or limbs, dull aches and lethargy. Phlegm is dampness which has congealed. Foods known to encourage dampness include, wheat, sugar, dairy produce, saturated fat, fruit juice, bananas and peanuts. Foods recommended to drain dampness include aduki beans, alfalfa, barley, black pepper, cayenne pepper, celery, corn, cinnamon, dill seed, fennel, garlic, horseradish, kidney beans, lemon, lentils, lettuce, marjoram, mushrooms, mustard, nutmeg, onions, parsley, pumpkin, radish, rye, spring (green) onions, turnips and walnuts.

Where food originates from gives us some clues to its energy value. For instance, millet is a grain which is grown in countries such as Africa where it is hot. Millet has a cooling energy to counteract this heat. Oats grow in northern climates and have a warming energy to balance the effects of the cooler conditions. There is therefore some sense in eating foods primarily from the country in which we live and primarily in the seasons in which they grow. However, life, or more especially eating, would be very boring if we took away all the foods that are now imported or grown in heated conditions such as bananas, mangoes, avocados and winter salads. The answer is not to deny ourselves the

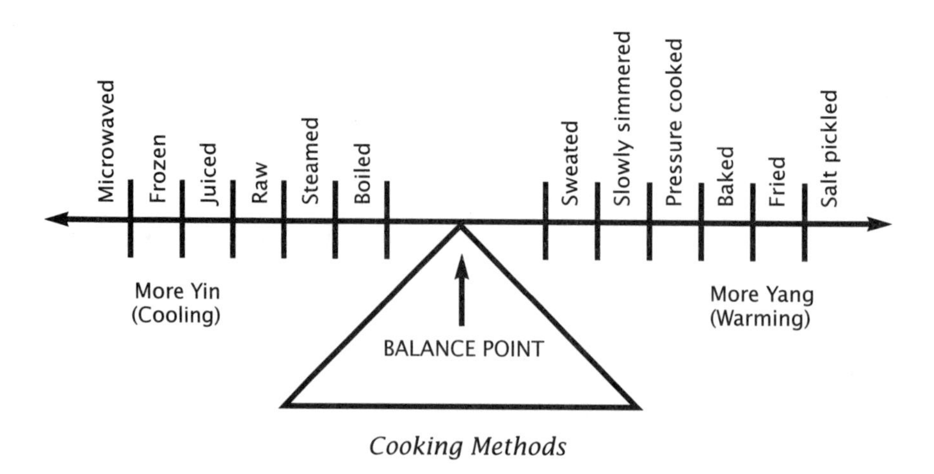

Cooking Methods

delights of such a varied diet but to balance it carefully by being aware of food energies. It is not sensible in the middle of winter (unless one is trying to counteract too much heat) to eat lots of salads or cold fruit juices. But provided we eat these occasionally and balance them by including warming foods or warming ways of cooking then we will stay healthy.

The way we cook food also has an influence on its energy. The diagram above shows how we can make food more warm and yang or cool and yin by the way it is cooked or prepared.

The above is a brief introduction to the energetics of food. Further information can be obtained from the wealth of books on Chinese medicine which are starting to appear in the bookshops. Some of these are listed in the appendix.

Yin and Yang

Another way of looking at the Chinese concept is in the consideration of yin and yang. We are all born with our own balance of yin and yang and in order to stay in good health we need to keep both these forces in balance. The food we eat is a major contributing factor in whether our bodies or moods become too yin or too yang. Yin foods and lifestyles fuel the mental, psychological or spiritual activity, the ability to relax, be mellow and flow or to be creative and intuitive. Over consumption of yin foods, however, can produce extreme yin symptoms such as feeling 'spaced-out', dreamy, fearful, worried, confused, forgetful, sad, oversensitive, ungrounded and lacking in will power. Yang foods fuel physical activity, the ability to get up and go, have purpose, be focused and clear thinking. However, over consumption of yang foods can create extreme yang symptoms such as compulsive, driven, controlling, stubborn behaviour with impatience, insensitivity, tightness, anger and resentment.

Centuries ago in the East it was the tradition to feed a vegetarian diet to those involved in religion or education and meat to those involved in war and manual work. Similarly, nowadays it is not always healthy for an individual to be vegetarian if they are having trouble getting their life together because they feel spaced-out with no will power or energy. The other extreme is a large percentage of the population who can't sit still. They are forceful, hard working and ambitious and

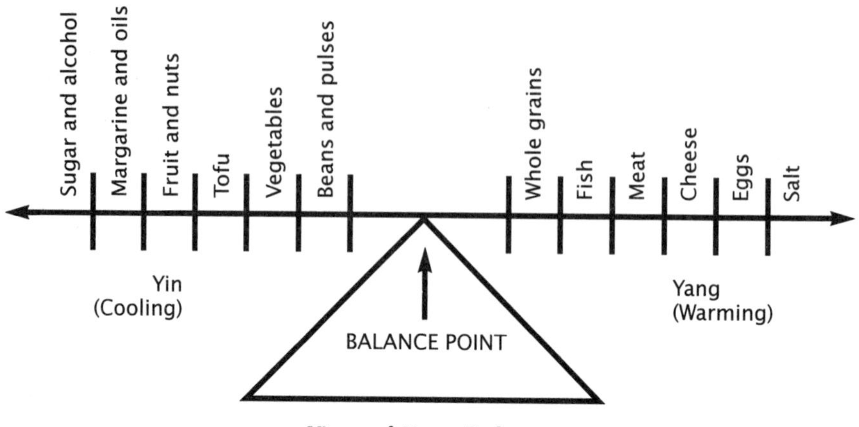

Yin and Yang Balance

would benefit from a more vegetarian diet in order to be more healthy, balanced and relaxed.

The chart above shows where foods lie on a see-saw between yin and yang. Foods at one extreme will often create cravings for foods at the other extreme to balance. However, a steady diet of extreme foods will lead to ill health, whereas a steady diet of foods in the middle, with the occasional use of foods from each end, will renew health and energy.

Our lifestyles can also have an effect on our yin and yang balance. Individuals who are too yang need to slow down, learn to relax or meditate, take time out just 'to be' or to read and need to learn to exercise self restraint. Yin individuals can make themselves more yang with exercise and activity, by being more involved and keeping warm.

The Menopause, Pre Menstrual Syndrome (PMS) and Candida

I learn so much from my own health problems and those of my patients that I sometimes feel that I need to be grateful for the symptoms that help me to understand and unravel ill health. The menopause has been one of these areas of discovery that has given me new insights, provided I have been prepared to look and listen. Most individuals' understanding of the menopause is about hot flushes and irregular periods and the idea is that the menopause starts as periods end. Through experience, I am starting to realise that the menopause starts approximately seven years before periods cease, and that the worst of the symptoms which many women face are during this period while the hormone levels are dropping. Once they have dropped, the worst is often over with. The symptoms appearing during this time are so varied that they are rarely recognised as being anything to do with the menopause.

This time of life is a transition period for women. It is the end of the childbearing era and a time to let go, not only of the restriction that childbearing brings, but any other restrictions which prevent them tapping into their own power and potential. The menopause is not only about working through any physical symptoms which a drop in hormones creates, but also about working through any mental or emotional issues which may emerge. If we can face our own fears and anxieties, angers and sorrows, we can find a place of peace deep within where we can hear the voice of our own soul. This voice encourages us to go within and find a balance between our animus and anima or yin and yang; a balance between drive and achievement and caring and nurturing.

In the past, women held men's feminine psyche and men held women's masculine psyche. Women nurtured and men achieved. This has changed over the years as women decided to reclaim their own power or animus and go out into the world to forge a career, but this has not been an easy transition for either because men have been reluctant to own their feminine psyche. The result has been an increase in the divorce rate mainly instigated by women who are often trying to be superwomen, holding down important jobs, looking after a family and home and still trying to be attractive, interesting human beings. Others who instigate divorce are battling to be themselves and achieve their potential but are being tied to the kitchen sink by men who fear their women's independence.

Future generations will not have the same problems that women in their forties and fifties are now facing. Young men are much more in touch with their feminine side, and young girls are not going to give up their prospects just to nurture others. The in-between generations are facing a transition which is part of the evolution of mankind but which often comes to a head around the time of the menopause when the body starts to eliminate emotional toxicity. Women need to use their animus, or masculine side, to stand up for themselves rather than to be hard on themselves trying to be superwomen and their anima, or feminine side, to care for themselves rather than just to nurture others. Many successful women, who appear to have everything, admit that they feel out of sync with themselves. They may be achieving but there is no time left to care for or to nurture themselves. Many women who have spent their lives caring for others suddenly feel that they want to find their own potential, to own their own voice and to break free from the imprisonment which they have accepted as normal. It is up to each person to find their own balance between the masculine and feminine by being still enough to listen to their inner guidance.

The menopause is not a disease but an opportunity to grow, to clear out all those things that are preventing us from finding our uniqueness, from reaching our creativity, power and potential. It is important to be open to needed changes, to own our fears and depression or our anxiety and anger. These are *our issues, our toxicity* and working through them enables us to succeed in realising our dreams. Changing our diets to a detoxification regime enables these issues to be worked on, as do other alternative therapies, books and workshops.

Pre Menstrual Syndrome (PMS) is like a mini menopause each month. When women say they could 'kill' before their period, it is their own anger rising to the surface. When women feel tearful around the time of a period it is *their tears*. By treating it as a disease which has a power over us, there is a tendency to blame PMS rather than looking for the causes of our pent-up emotions. Often the tears or anger are misplaced rather than being dealt with; for instance we may get angry at the children because of the mess they have created when really we are angry at our husbands for not supporting us more. We may cry over a film when really we are sad for ourselves because we don't nurture our feminine side sufficiently. Periods enable us to release our toxicity – physical, mental and emotional – on a monthly basis. The more we work through each month the less we will need to work through when the menopause comes along.

As well as being an emotional challenge, the menopause brings many physical symptoms to the fore. Below is a list of the most common menopausal symptoms.

MENOPAUSAL SYMPTOMS

Fatigue/lethargy
Headaches
Memory loss
Poor concentration
Dizzy spells
Confusion
Indecisiveness
Lack of motivation
Fearfulness
Phobias
Panic attacks
Lack of confidence
Anxiety
Irritability
Mood swings
Depression
Palpitations
Nausea
Weight gain
Insomnia
Night sweats
Hot flushes
Vaginal dryness
Changes in libido
Hair loss
Aches and pains
Dry skin
Itchy skin
Digestive problems
Flatulence
Bloating
Food allergies
Thrush
Vaginal discharge
Cystitis
Spots
Alternating constipation and diarrhoea
Urinary stress incontinence

If you look at the above list and compare it with the list on page 7 'A day in the life of your blood sugar' you will see that many symptoms are the same. During the onset of monthly periods it is a drop in blood sugar which causes headaches and lethargy and cravings for sweet and starchy food. Low blood sugar also allows the toxin levels to rise allowing feelings such as anger, negativity or depression to rise to the surface. What is happening is that lower levels of hormones, such as oestrogen and progesterone, encourage blood sugar to drop. Individuals with healthy blood sugar levels will experience minor symptoms of tiredness or hunger whilst those already suffering from low blood sugar will experience more severe symptoms related to very low blood sugar. During the menopause this drop in hormones is happening on a more permanent basis and so the symptoms of low blood sugar are around for longer. It is therefore very important during this time to eat the right kind of food at regular intervals in order to support the blood sugar. The lack of energy caused by low blood sugar can create a build-up of toxicity in the body and can lead to aches and pains, depression, hot sweats or a worsening of already present symptoms. It is difficult to separate symptoms and their causes because so many overlap each other. Depression could be caused by emotional toxicity that hasn't been dealt with in the past, but will be made worse by low blood sugar or toxicity building up. What I am trying to outline here is not an answer to every menopausal symptom but a new way of looking at the symptoms in order that each person can unravel their own picture.

My own, and my patients' journeys through the menopausal years and my search for answers to problems led me to Chinese medicine. This fascinating area of study is so holistic in its approach. It combines the reasons for physical, mental and emotional problems by talking about the effects of being too damp or cold or dry or hot etc. During the menopause our bodies are susceptible to becoming too damp or too dry (kidney yin or yang deficiency) due to the dropping hormone levels. Those who manage to keep a perfect balance will get away with fewer symptoms.

The weakening of the kidney yang by the dropping hormone levels encourages fluid retention in our cells or a state of dampness. We may not be aware of this dampness, as it may not be apparent. Fluid retention and weight gain are two symptoms of dampness but it can also affect one's ability to be enthusiastic or motivated or it can create a tendency to worry or be obsessive. It can be responsible for joint or muscle pain, urinary incontinence and fatigue. Dampness weakens the spleen and a weak spleen is then not only unable to transform excess dampness but its immune capacity is also reduced. This opens the door for a Candida invasion as Candida not only loves a weak immune system it also loves a damp environment and so a 'knock on' effect from being too damp is another list of symptoms often attributed to the menopause but really related to Candida overgrowth. These include digestive problems, diarrhoea, alternating constipation and diarrhoea, abdominal bloating and flatulence, indigestion, vaginal discharge, thrush, cystitis, spots, skin rashes, fungal infections etc. A similar effect can be seen around the time of their periods when women will often experience some of these symptoms due to their bodies holding on to fluid and the dampness encouraging Candida overgrowth. The emotional effects of dampness, such as negative feelings, further the weakening of the immune system as the immune system responds to joy and laughter rather than depression and negativity.

Dietary changes can help to alleviate symptoms related to dampness and Candida. *Cooking Without* not only discourages Candida but it raises the blood sugar or energy levels in order that the body can function better on every level. In the oriental section is a list of food energies and this includes a list of damp encouraging foods most of which are avoided when cooking without. By limiting these foods and increasing the use of damp-removing foods, improvements in health will be seen. Additionally, those suffering from kidney yang deficiency could increase their intake of yang foods and yang cooking methods. Exercise is also a yang activity.

Kidney yin deficiency creates symptoms more synonymous with the menopause and because of this they are more likely to be attributed to the menopause than kidney yang deficiency symptoms. Kidney yin deficiency encourages heat and dryness which leads to dry skin, dry eyes, constipation and hot flushes. There may be an irregular cycle or unpredictable flow as well as hyperactivity, tension, palpitations or anxiety. Diet wise these individuals will also benefit from raising their blood sugar levels as the increase in energy will assist the body in coping with the changes taking place. Avoiding food allergens will often help to alleviate hot flushes as will detoxification, as the body is often trying to overflow its toxicity through the skin. Eating more salads, fruits and cooling foods, as listed in the section on oriental medicine, will also benefit kidney yin deficiency.

Hopefully, this section will have given you some new insights into the menopause and PMS and opened up new areas of understanding. There is no way a book such as this can have an answer to everyone's health problems. It is my intention to spur people on to find their own solutions by looking at diet and nutrition and by finding assistance from therapists, health food shops and books (some of which I have listed in the appendix).

Allergies and Intolerances

Only a few individuals suffer from allergies but many suffer from intolerances. True allergies cause obvious symptoms such as swellings, rashes, pain, blisters etc. Intolerances, however, create a stress on the body that lowers the blood sugar and undermines health. Intolerances may not be apparent until the offending foods are removed from the diet. Symptoms of ill health may then disappear only to reappear when the offending food is re-introduced. Intolerances have a part to play in all major disease states. I have explained allergies and intolerances in my first book, but below are some new areas of understanding and new ways of looking at the reasons for food sensitivities.

The Chinese view of allergies is that we are too damp. Dampness in the digestive tract prevents food being well digested – it puts out the digestive fire. This means that food residues then travel too far down the digestive tract where they encourage the proliferation of bad intestinal flora such as Candida. Candida, which is naturally present in our digestive tract, is not encouraged if the only substance to reach the large intestine is the fibre left from food. However, if Candida is well fed with food residues, it will break through the intestinal wall into the blood stream where it will meet the immune system. This results in the immune system over-reacting and producing allergies or intolerances. Other individuals may not be aware of symptoms related to Candida overgrowth or food sensitivities until some time in the future when they develop a more serious illness. It is possible that most serious illnesses start with a problem in the digestive tract and research is starting to implicate this in conditions such as autism and cancer.

Allergies and intolerances can be overcome, provided we are prepared to work sufficiently hard to rebuild our health. Food sensitivities leave the immune system open to toxicity entering into it from the digestive tract and this toxicity in turn weakens the immune system and leaves it even more vulnerable. The answer to allergies and intolerances lies in detoxifying the body of any physical, mental or emotional toxicity in order that the immune system is better able to cope. Alongside this the digestive tract needs to be clean, healed and functioning well.

Behind every allergy or intolerance lies the mental and emotional reason for its presence. Allergies and intolerances are about us denying our existence. In the case of total allergy syndrome when individuals are living a very restricted lifestyle because they are allergic to so many substances they are denying their existence to the point where they may die. Often this denial is based on our fears. Because of our lack of self-worth we deny our right to be happy, healthy, successful, free etc.

but it is our fears which prevent us from overcoming the obstacles that our lack of self worth imposes upon us.

The speech attributed to Nelson Mandela sums this up brilliantly and I often hand this out to my patients to give them food for thought.

'Our deepest fear is not that we are inadequate. Our deepest fear is that we are powerful beyond measure. It is our light, not our darkness that most frightens us. We ask ourselves, "Who am I to be brilliant, gorgeous, talented, fabulous?" Actually, who are you not to be? You are a child of God. Your playing small doesn't serve the world. There's nothing enlightened about shrinking so that other people won't feel insecure around you. We are all meant to shine, as children do – and as we let our light shine, we unconsciously give other people permission to do the same. As we are liberated from our own fear, our presence automatically liberates others'.

The more allergic or intolerant we become, the more difficult it may seem to overcome our fears and reach our potential in life. And this is in fact the case. What is happening in life is that somewhere in the past we were sent an obstacle to overcome – like a molehill to climb. If our fears or lack of self-worth prevent our overcoming this obstacle then the universe says, 'OK, you ignored that obstacle so here's a bigger one to overcome, you can't ignore this one'. But alas we often do. In other words our allergies and intolerances are our power turned inwards – the more we deny our power and existence the more likely we are to have food sensitivities. Eventually, we end up with a mountain rather than a molehill to climb. We have collected a mountain of issues that we have been avoiding facing and it is only by working through these issues that eventually we will not be allergic to food or life.

There is a tendency when we become aware of food sensitivities to allow them to have power over us. We become fearful about what we eat or of not being able to find the right food to eat. Our allergies and intolerances control us and control our life. It is as though our fears about life have been transferred to our food and existence, and we try to control, while feeling more and more out of control. Healing starts when we relax and accept where we are at this moment in time, including our ill health. It's about loving ourselves, and loving our condition. It's about letting go of control and learning to have faith in a higher power. It's about being prepared to work to make changes but accepting that we are human and make mistakes.

It is necessary to avoid certain foods, especially if these cause allergic reactions but this should not be made into a negative experience. Rather than looking at denying food and breeding fear we need to look at making food enjoyable, something to look forward to and something which builds health. We need to keep our diets as varied as possible within its limitations to prevent further food sensitivities appearing. This means that we need to put more emphasis on food and feeding ourselves on a daily basis. By eating the right kind of diet our body is able to detoxify itself of not only the physical toxicity which affects health, but also the mental and emotional causes of our allergies and intolerances.

The aim is to be able to say, 'I can eat anything I want to. I just happen to choose to eat sensibly but I am not afraid of food or of enjoying myself'. If we eat a food that is not good for us, it is better to give it to ourselves with love rather than with fear. In other words if we can't resist the ice cream or chocolate bar it is better to enjoy it rather than give ourselves a hard time about giving in to it or of fearing its consequences. Eventually, when we have learned to love ourselves sufficiently we will find it easy to choose the right foods for ourselves because we care.

Our mental attitude is so important with any disease but it is very important in the case of allergies and intolerances. Just as one person who has been told they will die in three weeks dutifully fulfils the prediction, and another, by being positive and refusing to go, denies it, so we too can affect our response to food sensitivities by our mental attitude. My son provides a good example of this. Having spent a few months camping on the continent one summer he came home with digestive problems. His diet had consisted largely of bread. I sent him for an allergy test and needless to say he was allergic to wheat. However, because he was still at university and cutting out wheat restricted his life, he decided to ignore the recommendations. His diet was generally good with lots of fruit and vegetables and his mental attitude was very positive. His digestive problems eventually disappeared and two years later a test showed that he no longer had a wheat allergy.

In other words, we can say goodbye to allergies and intolerances with the right mental attitude but, alas, few of us have the ability to be strong enough or have sufficient faith to do this with immediate effect. Often in my own journey in life I have felt that I have taken an enormous detour in order to learn certain lessons, which suddenly seem very simple having reached the other side. In other words, if I could have made the mental shift required I wouldn't have needed to go the long way round. Allergies and intolerances are like this, we have lots to learn from them but only *we* can decide whether we are capable of taking short cuts or whether we need to go the long way round.

On a practical level, it is impossible for me to write a book where everyone's allergies and intolerances are dealt with. However, it is quite easy to use substitutions in many recipes. I do have a tendency to use lots of onions in savoury dishes because they give such a good flavour. If you cannot tolerate onions then omit them or use another vegetable in their place. Aubergine (eggplant) makes a good substitute, especially in recipes where onions are puréed to produce a creamy texture. Sweet potatoes or parsnips can be used instead of carrots, carrot or vegetable juice instead of canned or sieved tomatoes. Parsnips can replace potatoes. It is possible in some recipes to replace eggs with egg substitutes. Flours can be substituted in baked goods. Try millet flour instead of rice flour and gram flour instead of soya flour. Rice milk can be used instead of soya milk though it is not quite as stable when heated and does separate a little sometimes. I have used dates as a sweetening agent in puddings and cakes but for those intolerant of dried fruit a new product called stevia made from a South American herb can be substituted (see page 43). Be inventive and don't be frightened of making mistakes. A lot of mistakes went into making *Vegetarian Cooking Without* and I ate most of them!

Weight Control

Eating well is not only the answer to staying healthy, it is also the answer to weight control. Forget crash diets and counting calories, weight control is not about starving the body but about feeding it the right kind of food at regular intervals. When you reduce your intake as part of a diet the body thinks there is a famine. Because it's not sure where the next meal is coming from it slows down the metabolism to get the best use of the food it is receiving. In practice, I find that 95% of my patients lose weight even if they don't have much excess. While losing this weight they are spending time feeding themselves more than they have probably eaten in a long time. So what is happening?

First of all, I insist that all my patients eat six meals per day. These are not tiny portions but consist of the right kind of food (dairy-free, sugar-free, wheat-free etc.) with substantial amounts of complex carbohydrates and vegetables. The reason I insist on six meals per day is to improve blood sugar or energy levels in order that the body can start to remove toxicity. A knock-on effect from raising the blood sugar is that the metabolism speeds up and individuals burn up not only the food they are eating but the excess they are carrying as well.

Metabolism can be likened to a burning fire. If we want to burn a lot of waste material it is best not to put it all on at once or there is a likelihood that the fire will smoulder and struggle and probably leave a lot of unburned debris. However, if the fire is fed smaller amounts of waste at regular intervals, suddenly, the pile of refuse has gone and there is very little residue.

Secondly, my diet reduces sugar intake and refined carbohydrate consumption. Sugary foods and refined carbohydrates, which are broken down quickly into simple sugars, lead to an increase in the output of the hormone insulin. Insulin takes excess sugar out of the bloodstream and stores it as fat. Excess sugar in the blood stream therefore means excess insulin output, which in turn means weight gain. Stimulants such as coffee, cola, chocolate and alcohol also increase the levels of circulating insulin by kicking the adrenal glands into releasing blood sugar. Some people – for whom sugar creates nervous energy – are exceptions to this rule as they tend to burn up energy by being hyperactive. They may not be storing weight (and in fact are often slim) and so are unaware of the damage sugary foods are doing to their nervous system.

Food sensitivities can also play a part in weight gain or an inability to lose weight. The immune system releases chemical mediators of inflammation in response to food sensitivity or allergy and the resulting oedema causes weight gain. Any food can cause problems but it is often the food or foods we crave the most which are the culprits. Over the last few centuries, geographical movement has meant that specific racial groups who have not had the exposure to certain foods (for example milk) have not evolved the genetic disposition to tolerate them. Food sensitivities are also encouraged by advances in food technology – such as new processing and preserving methods and the use of food additives – which have altered food to the point that it can cause disruption to the immune system when it is no longer recognised as food. Further complications can arise from the overuse of antibiotics, coupled with the increased consumption of refined carbohydrates and sugars. These cause an overgrowth of Candida, which in turn encourages 'leaky gut syndrome'. A leaky gut allows incompletely digested food particles to enter the blood stream where they trigger an immune response or food sensitivity. Incomplete digestion of food is also encouraged by modern methods of food preparation, which destroy foods' natural enzyme content.

Finally, if we look at weight control from a Chinese point of view it is the spleen and kidney which govern metabolic processes. An overweight person has two problems – fat and water. It is the essential yang or fire that activates and supports all the transformational processes. Fire can burn fat and turn water into steam. If, however, the fire or yang of the kidneys and spleen becomes depressed or insufficient, the ability to maintain a consistent level of energy and a stable balance of fat, fluid and flesh becomes undermined. On the other hand, overactive yang or fire induces an increase of metabolic activity which can result in loss of fat and muscle mass. Increasing the burning fire of the kidneys and spleen in order to burn-up excess fat and water can be achieved by making one's diet, one's methods of cooking and one's lifestyle more yang. See the section on Yin and Yang on page 17.

Weight control is, as you can see, multifaceted and complex. However, by changing one's diet it is obviously possible to become slim and fit without ever resorting to counting calories or starving oneself. Weight is ultimately linked with health and eating a diet to build health is the best way to obtain control.

Balancing a Vegetarian or Vegan Diet

Eating a balanced vegetarian diet isn't difficult but neither is it quite as easy as when one consumes meat. Cutting out certain foods and becoming a vegetarian or vegan is not the answer to health problems. What is important is the quality of the foods we include, not what we cut out. A diet without flesh needs compensating for with vegetarian alternatives. Meat is a rich source of protein, iron and B12, so we need to look for alternative sources of these nutrients.

Protein

Nobody needs huge amounts of protein from any source. Growing children and pregnant women need a little more. Protein is essential for cell growth, for tissue repair and for reproduction but our daily requirements are quite small. Protein is made up of 23 different amino acids. We can make many of them in our bodies by converting other amino acids, but eight cannot be made; they have to be provided in the diet and so they are called essential amino acids. Protein from animal sources, meat, eggs, fish, milk, cheese etc. provides all eight essential amino acids and is therefore termed 'complete'. Individual plant foods do not contain all the essential amino acids we need in the right proportions, but when we mix plant foods together, any deficiency in one is cancelled out by an excess in the other. We mix foods to produce protein all the time, whether we are meat eaters or vegetarians. It is a normal part of the human way of eating. Examples include beans on toast and rice and dahl.

Food combining to obtain these essential amino acids needn't be complicated. By following a few basic principles and eating foods from two or more of the following groups, plenty of protein will be available to the body.

NUTS AND SEEDS
Sunflower, sesame, pumpkin, linseeds, brazils, pecans, hazelnuts, almonds, walnuts, cashews, pine nuts

BEANS AND PULSES
Peanuts, peas, beans, lentils and products made from soya beans such as tofu and soya milk

GRAINS
Oats, corn, wheat, rye, barley, millet, quinoa, buckwheat, rice

It is now known that the body has a pool of amino acids so that if one meal is deficient, it can be made up, to a certain extent, from the body's own stores. Because of this we do not need to be obsessive about complementing amino acids all the time as long as our diet is generally varied and well balanced. Vegans need to take a little more care than vegetarians because they do not obtain complete proteins from any individual constituent of their diet, whereas vegetarians will obtain some complete proteins from eggs or dairy produce.

B12

Vitamin B12 is essential for the formation of healthy red blood cells; deficiency causes a form of anaemia. As it is found only in animal foods (with the exception of uncertain amounts in seaweed and fermented soya products) it is the vitamin most likely to be lacking in a vegetarian or, more especially, a vegan diet. Vegetarians who consume eggs will get sufficient from these. Traditional vegans and vegetarians in countries such as India do not seem to have a problem obtaining B12 from their diet. It is quite possible that these indigenous people, whose diets have not been adulterated by western food, are able to manufacture B12 from intestinal flora in their digestive tract. Alternatively B12 can be manufactured from bacteria on fresh garden vegetables and fermented foods, but in the west, due to the intensive processing of fruit and vegetables by the food industry, we can no longer rely on these products as adequate sources of B12. Vegans should be careful to include some fortified foods (such as soya milk) in their diet or use a supplement of B12 if necessary.

Iron

Iron is readily found in meat but can easily be obtained by vegetarians and vegans from pulses, soya products, green vegetables, whole grain cereals, dried fruit, nuts and seeds. The iron in these foods will be maximised if they are eaten with foods containing vitamin C, such as fruit and vegetables.

Calcium

In general, we are led to believe that we do not obtain sufficient calcium if we do not consume milk and dairy produce. However, calcium is readily available in foods such as green leafy vegetables, fruit, nuts, seeds, dried fruit, pulses and whole grains. Because meat contains high levels of phosphorus which depletes calcium levels, vegetarians and vegans often have better levels of calcium in their bodies than omnivores.

Fat

Children need more fat in their diets than adults. Vegetarian children can obtain these levels with the help of milk products and eggs but care needs to be taken with vegan children to make sure the levels which they obtain are sufficient. Good vegan sources of fat include nut and seed butters, vegetable oils and avocados.

Why gluten-free, yeast-free, sugar-free, saturated fat-free and dairy-free?

My intention when putting patients on a therapeutic dietary regime is to address certain issues in order that the body can regain its health. So why is this dietary regime free from wheat, yeast, sugar, saturated fat and dairy produce? Although not all my patients are prevented from eating all the above, in writing a recipe book I have tried to produce recipes to cover every situation. Generally my intention is to remove the main foods that cause sensitivities, as well as removing those foods which suppress toxicity from being eliminated. I also aim to limit foods which cause undue stress on the body's energy levels when being digested, and foods which don't add nutritionally to the body. It is then necessary to replace these foods with ones that are high in nutrients and fibre and are easy to digest. In my first recipe book, I give detailed explanations about the above foods but below is a brief summary, together with an update of new information. The length of time for which problem foods should be avoided will depend on the severity of one's ill health. It may be a few months or a few years. Once work has been done on improving health, try widening the range of foods consumed. When reintroducing foods, try one new food at a time to see its effects and be prepared to go back to a stricter regime if the body is still not ready to cope.

Gluten

Gluten is present in wheat, rye, oats and barley. Sometimes people are intolerant of the gluten in all these foods, other individuals may have an intolerance to one or more but not necessarily all of them. Others may not be allergic to gluten but have a problem with the grains. Wheat is one of the most common foods to which people react. Wheat also has a suppressive action on the body's ability to eliminate toxicity. If you look at the sliding scale diagram on balancing elimination (on page 4) you will see that wheat sits on the left hand side. Even with patients who do not have a wheat allergy or intolerance I always drastically reduce its intake. The more ill they are the more likely that wheat will be removed altogether. The widespread use of wheat in our diets together with the fact that many strains of wheat now grown are new varieties which our bodies have not learnt to adapt to, means that many people nowadays are finding that they have an intolerance to wheat and wheat products. Some individuals who cannot tolerate modern wheat can cope well with spelt flour, which comes from a very old strain of wheat that has been around since Roman times.

Rye, oats and barley are often tolerated better than wheat because they are less likely to have been overused. Their use does help to add interest and variety to the diet if they are acceptable foods.

Yeast

Yeast is a food that causes intolerance in many people. Yeast is implicated in candida problems (see my first book for more information on candida). There is, however, still quite a lot of controversy on what constitutes a yeast food. Macrobiotics insist that miso and shoyu sauce are good for the intestinal flora while others say the yeast in bread has been killed so isn't a problem. I think that each case is individual and it is only by trial and error that suitable foods can be determined. Some of this individuality is related to whether the problem is caused by yeast intolerance or a problem with candida. In the first instance an intolerance or allergy will cause a reaction when only a small amount of yeast, or yeast-related foods, are eaten, whether the yeast has been killed by heat or not. Candida problems, on the other hand, will be encouraged by eating too many yeasted foods or by foods not being sufficiently well digested so that they reach the large intestine as food for the candida.

This book aims to supply recipes which are free from added yeast, although I have included dried fruit and mushrooms which may still cause a problem for some individuals. Hopefully, there are sufficient recipes without these to enable a varied diet. Yeast related foods include yeast extract, vinegar, citric acid, monosodium glutamate, stock cubes, alcohol, cheese, mushrooms, dried fruit, miso, shoyu or tamari sauce (soya sauce).

Sugar

Sugar is one food which I never recommend my patients to reintroduce, however well they feel. Sugar has too many negative aspects. The aim of detoxification is to improve health and strengthen the immune system so that foods originally causing problems may be eaten once more. However, sugar, especially in a processed form, is an immune system suppressor. Research has shown that eating 100 grams of sugar per day causes the immune system response to be reduced by 50–60%. It wouldn't take long for a decline in health to follow its reintroduction.

Sugary foods also rob the body of energy, vitamins and minerals each time they are eaten. Too much sugar in the blood stream is dangerous and causes the pancreas to produce insulin for its removal. This not only uses energy from the body to perform this task but it also robs the body of vitamins and minerals, which are used to produce insulin. Sugar removed from the blood stream is then stored as fat in the cells for future use, but if not used, its deposition causes weight gain.

Sugar encourages the overgrowth of bad intestinal flora such as candida and is therefore best avoided in any processed form. Sugar in the form of fruit should be limited to two pieces per day though people with severe candida, may need to limit this still further. Excessive fruit consumption also pulls too much toxicity out of the cells and makes individuals more yin (see Yin and Yang page 17). Fruit juices, because they contain concentrated fruit sugars, should also be avoided or severely limited.

Dairy Produce

Unfortunately, many individuals who decide to become vegetarians do so by substituting dairy produce for meat and fish. It is rare to find good cookery books, or restaurants, whose vegetarian dishes do not contain cheese, cream or milk. However, dairy produce is not necessarily a healthier option than meat or fish. Milk is for babies. Human babies are meant to drink their mother's milk, cows' milk is for their calves. Many individuals are now intolerant of milk and milk products and those who are not, will find milk and its products encourage the production of catarrh and acidity. Once milk products have been eliminated, improvements in health will often be seen. Milk is one of those foods which I don't encourage individuals to put back in their diets in quantity once health has been obtained.

Saturated Fat

Fats can be categorised into saturates, polyunsaturates and monounsaturates. Eating a vegetarian diet automatically cuts down on saturated fat consumption and encourages the use of unsaturated fats in such foods as oils, beans, vegetables, seeds and nuts. My first volume of *Cooking Without* explains fats in more detail but generally we need to balance our intake of linoleic fatty acids and linolenic fatty acids. Linolenic fatty acids found in green vegetables, linseeds and linseed oil (plus fish if eaten) are easily unbalanced if too much linoleic acid is consumed in the form of polyunsaturated vegetable oils and margarines. It is generally safest to eat polyunsaturated fats mainly in their natural food form rather than oils and margarines. The best oil to use is olive oil, a monounsaturate with certain health-giving properties. It is also important that our diets contain sufficient fat to encourage the gall bladder to empty. The gall bladder, which stores toxicity eliminated from the liver, is emptied in response to fat in the digestive tract so it is not a good idea to eat a fat-free diet.

Salt

I have included salt in the recipes in this book but not in my first volume of *Cooking Without*. This is partly for my own sanity as preparing salt-free vegetarian recipes is more difficult than salt-free recipes where meat or fish is included. But it is also because I feel that salt can be part of a balanced diet if used in small quantities. I think that it is a good idea to avoid salt for 3–4 months in order to learn to taste food.

This is hard to do as our palettes have become so adulterated with salty, unnaturally- flavoured food that at first food tastes very bland when salt is removed. However, we eventually start to taste the food rather than the salt. It is then safe to start adding a little salt to those dishes which need a little to bring out the flavour, such as soups and casseroles. Salt is not needed on the table or in cooked vegetables or grains.

The Do's and Don'ts of Detoxification

Vegetarian Cooking Without can be used as a recipe book for individuals looking for vegetarian and vegan meals and also for those on restricted eating regimes. *Vegetarian Cooking Without* can also be used to assist detoxification. Two of the main causes of health problems are toxicity and malnutrition; we may be well fed but often we are undernourished. Toxicity is a continual threat to our health and is not something which we can completely avoid. Toxins are present in our food, in the air we breathe and the water we drink. Toxins come from any drugs or alcohol we imbibe, from cigarette smoke, household chemicals and from any emotions we haven't dealt with in our lives. *Vegetarian Cooking Without* encourages the use of sufficient quantities of nutrient-rich foods in order to build health. At the same time, by eating a diet free from added wheat, dairy produce, sugar, yeast and saturated fat, the body will automatically start to detoxify. Include the following foods in a detoxification regime:

EGGS
Up to seven eggs per week are acceptable, preferably organically produced.

VEGETABLES
Approximately 40% of food consumed should be in the form of vegetables. Each day, aim to eat a large, varied salad and a good selection of cooked vegetables as well as vegetarian savouries. Try to vary the vegetables and use, where possible, those in season. Sweet peppers, aubergines (eggplant), potatoes and tomatoes should be eaten in moderation because they contain more natural toxins than other vegetables. Mushrooms may need to be limited or avoided if a Candida problem is

present and spinach should not be eaten in excess because it is high in oxalic acid which binds with minerals such as calcium. Aim to buy organically-grown produce whenever possible.

BEANS AND PULSES

These are good sources of protein for vegetarians and vegans. Include in soups, casseroles, bakes and salads etc.

NUTS AND SEEDS

Nuts and seeds are good sources of protein for vegetarians and vegans but they are best used moderately, as nuts are high in fat and not too easy to digest. Try nut roasts as well as nut and seed butters. Avoid salted nuts and peanuts.

RICE

Rice is the ideal food to keep the blood sugar stable while soaking up toxic waste from the body. Preferably use short-grain, organically-grown brown rice. You can use rice without limit, but each day aim to consume between 125–285g/4–10oz/½–1½ cups uncooked weight.

BUCKWHEAT, MILLET AND QUINOA

These grains can be used instead of, or as well as, rice in the form of whole grains or flakes.

CORN

Corn can be used as flour for baking or as a thickening agent and in the form of sweetcorn as a vegetable.

OATS, BARLEY AND RYE

These grains do contain gluten but can be useful to add variety to the diet provided that they do not cause food sensitivities. They can be used in the form of oatcakes, rye crispbreads, porridge, muesli, etc.

FRUIT

Limit fruit to one or two pieces per day. Avoid fresh fruit juice or substitute one small glass of fruit juice for two pieces of fruit. Limit tropical fruits and very acidic fruits such as oranges, grapefruit, lemons, plums and strawberries. Whenever possible, eat fruit in season and fruit which has been organically grown. Fruit may need to be avoided in the early stages of treating Candida albicans.

DRIED FRUIT

Use in moderation, preferably unsulphured. Avoid in the early stages of treating Candida albicans, if you have an intolerance to yeast or suffer from flatulence or bloating.

BEVERAGES

Avoid tea, coffee, carbonated soft drinks, squashes, fruit juice and alcohol. Substitute with herb teas, rooibosch tea, coffee substitutes and filtered water. Beware of additives such as lactose and flavourings in some alternative drinks.

WATER INTAKE

Most individuals do not drink sufficient water to assist their body with its removal of waste products. Try to drink at least three to four pints of filtered or bottled water per day, preferably warm or at room temperature. Drink in between meals in order to prevent digestive juices being diluted.

Putting *Cooking Without* into practice

For at least the first three months of following this eating regime, I suggest that meals are eaten six times per day. This enables the body to obtain blood sugar or energy from food rather than from the release of adrenalin or from the liver's glycogen stores. The energy that comes from eating regularly will not only make you feel better but will also enable the internal organs and systems of the body to feel good and remove any toxic build-up.

Food may initially have to be forced into the body at regular intervals, as individuals with low blood sugar do not always feel like eating and can even feel sick at the thought of food. Once the blood sugar has been raised by the intake of food, the body seems grateful and will actually start asking to be fed at regular intervals. During this phase you need to make sure that you always have a snack with you wherever you are going in order to keep topping up the blood sugar. Miss the snack and let the blood sugar fall and you will spend the rest of the day feeling under par, chasing your blood sugar but never actually catching it up.

Eventually, when the body has removed excess toxins and obtained sufficient vitamins and minerals from the improved diet, three meals per day should be adequate, with an occasional snack such as a piece of fruit or some nuts in between. By then the liver should be supporting the blood sugar between meals, and adrenalin can be kept for emergency situations. Your body will tell you when you are ready for this; it may be in three months' time or it may be in two years' time, depending on the state of your health when you start detoxifying. Suddenly you will find that you are no longer ill and no longer feel hungry all the time.

Suggested Menus

BREAKFAST

See my first volume of *Cooking Without* for breakfast recipes such as soaked muesli, light muesli, rice porridge with cinnamon, cloves and dates; millet porridge with fresh fruit, nuts and seeds or egg fried rice.

MID-MORNING

Try eating rice served with fresh fruit and nuts, soup, or chopped salad vegetables. Alternatively, see the first courses section for pâtés to serve with rice cakes, or wheat-free crackers. If you cannot eat a substantial snack mid-morning, eat a second course to breakfast and some fresh fruit or nuts and seeds mid-morning.

LUNCH

Eat a substantial lunch such as home-made soup followed by a salad with a vegetarian savoury, rice, or baked potatoes.

MID-AFTERNOON

Include a substantial rice snack if you do not eat an evening meal until late. Otherwise, try rice cakes with nut butter and mashed banana or with avocado and tomato. Fresh fruit, nuts and seeds may be sufficient if eating an early evening meal or try baking some cakes or scones.

EVENING MEAL

A vegetarian savoury served with rice, millet, quinoa, wheat-free pasta, or potatoes, plus a selection of vegetables and/or a salad.

SUPPER

Eat a substantial supper unless you have eaten your evening meal late. Try porridge or other breakfast cereals, rice with fruit, soup and rice or pâtés with wheat-free crackers.

Make the change gradually

It is a good idea to start any new regime gradually, perhaps over a period of one to four weeks, depending on how good your diet is to start with. The body is used to coping with foods, such as meat, wheat, tea and coffee, which suppress the elimination of toxins and push them back into the cells. By removing or reducing such foods and increasing the amount of vegetables eaten, toxins are encouraged to flow out of the cells. If, however, they flow out of the cells faster than the body can eliminate them to the outside world, excess toxins float around in the bloodstream, making you feel worse rather than better. This may cause an upset stomach, headache, anxiety, tiredness, or can aggravate symptoms already present. It is also important that sufficient grains, such as rice, millet or quinoa, are eaten as these help to soak up excess toxins and assist with their removal. If you still feel any adverse reactions to the diet, then make the changeover more gradual but don't give up, your body is responding well by throwing off toxins so don't discourage it.

Organising Your Cooking

Do not think that *Cooking Without* is about denying food, rather that it is about building health. Try to organise your cooking so that you have lots of tempting dishes available when you open the refrigerator door. In this way you will not think about what you cannot eat but rather about what you can enjoy. It only takes a change in attitude to put food and feeding ourselves correctly at the top of our priority list for the day rather than at the bottom where it fits in if there is any time left.

It is a good idea to put aside a few hours, once or twice per week, in order to make a few dishes at the same time. If you are chopping vegetables for a casserole you may as well make a pan of soup or a curry. If you put the oven on to make a nut roast you may as well bake a cake. When cooked, decant some food into the freezer for use in emergency situations, or for use later in the week. Keep the remainder in the refrigerator so that for the next few days you have plenty to tempt you. It is a good idea to keep rice ready cooked (it will keep for two days but must be kept in the refrigerator) or frozen so that you only need to rustle up a salad or cook some vegetables to complete a meal.

Cooking Ingredients and Methods

Brown Rice

Some recipes call for cooked rice, others have quantities listed for uncooked rice. If you wish to substitute one for another you should note that rice approximately doubles in weight when cooked. Rice will keep for two days but must be stored in the refrigerator. It can also be frozen in containers, making it readily available. To defrost, decant into a sieve and pour boiling water through the rice. Most people have their own favourite way of cooking rice; here is mine.

Cooking Brown Rice

Soak 225g/8oz/1 cup brown rice in a pan with lots of cold water for approximately 10 minutes. This loosens any dirt on the rice and prevents any scum forming when it is cooked. Sieve the rice and place in a pan with 1.25 litres/40fl oz/5 cups) of boiling water. Bring to the boil and simmer until the rice is cooked, the length of time will depend on the type and batch of rice. Short grain brown rice will take between 30–40 minutes, whereas long grain will take approximately 20–25 minutes. There will still be lots of water left in the pan when the rice has cooked. Pour the rice and water into a sieve and allow it to drain. Serve hot or leave to cool in the sieve over the pan with the lid on to prevent the rice from drying out. A tupperware rice container is useful for both sieving and storing cooked rice.

Cooking Millet, Buckwheat and Quinoa

These grains can be used in recipes as an alternative to brown rice. To cook, follow the instructions for cooking brown rice, but cook buckwheat and quinoa for approximately 10 minutes and millet for approximately 18 minutes. Like rice, millet doubles in weight once cooked, buckwheat and quinoa treble in weight.

Cooking Beans

Cooking time depends on the age of the beans (old beans take longer), the size of the beans and the length of the soaking time. Smaller beans and pulses, such as lentils, mung beans, aduki beans and split peas, can be cooked without soaking. Larger beans need soaking overnight in plenty of water which has been brought to the boil. Discard the soaking water and rinse well before cooking. Even after soaking, large beans can take up to 2 hours to cook. This is where I find a pressure cooker invaluable as most large beans can be cooked in only 5 minutes after an overnight soak. They are not mushy at this stage but are ready to be placed in casseroles and soups. It is a good idea to boil all beans well for the first 10 minutes of cooking as some beans contain a toxin which is only destroyed at high temperatures. Beans approximately double in size when soaked and cooked.

Beans can be frozen at the soaked stage or the just-cooked stage so that a supply is always at hand. Try freezing them in a colander or sieve as this allows any excess water to drain away. The beans can then be tipped into a plastic bag where, with a little encouragement, they will become free flowing, allowing you to take out just the amount you need at any time. I always keep a few cans of beans in the cupboard and these are now becoming more acceptable as they can increasingly be bought without added salt and sugar. Canned beans do seem easier to digest and appear to cause less flatulence than the soaked and cooked beans.

Freezing Orange and Lemon – juice and rind

Neither of these juices should be used in large quantities as they cause excess elimination of toxins from the cells, which, if not removed by the body, can cause symptoms of ill health to appear. They are, however, ideal to use in small quantities to add flavour to recipes. I keep ice cubes made from orange and lemon juice in the freezer for such occasions. Orange and lemon rind can also be frozen, but preferably buy organically grown as most fruits will have been heavily sprayed. Grate the rind and loosely pack into small containers. If you cannot tolerate citrus fruits, then leave these flavourings out of recipes.

Freezing Ginger

Fresh ginger goes dry and mouldy quite quickly even if kept in the refrigerator. Peel a large piece of ginger and place in a plastic bag in the freezer. Whenever you need ginger for a recipe, grate a little of the frozen ginger and return the rest to the freezer. It is surprisingly easy to grate.

Freezing Herbs

I like to use fresh herbs whenever possible but the next best substitute is frozen herbs. Some supermarkets are now selling frozen herbs but it is cheaper to buy or grow and freeze your own. Wash and spin the herbs and finely chop (I use the food processor) and loosely pack in individual containers in the freezer.

MUSTARD
This is not an easy product to find without added vinegar or wheat but it is available as mustard flour with no other added ingredients and as English mustard with only salt added (see list of suppliers, page 212).

STEVIA – AN ALTERNATIVE SWEETENER
This South American shrub has leaves that taste very sweet and is known locally as 'Honey leaf'. Extracts of stevia are estimated to be up to 300 times sweeter than sugar, but stevia has no calories. In many countries stevia has been known for many years. Japan, in particular, has done extensive research and safety testing on the plant. The herb has been shown to be non-toxic and safe for diabetics and hypoglycaemics. In addition, stevia does not nourish the bacteria in the mouth, as sugars do, nor does it stimulate the growth of Candida in the digestive tract.

Stevia can be supplied as a powdered or liquid extract, or as pure powdered leaf (see list of suppliers, page 212). I have used the powdered extract in some of the cake and pudding recipes in this book to enable those individuals with a dried fruit intolerance to have some treats. Although it does have a sweet taste it also has a distinctive aftertaste and needs to be used in very small quantities and in recipes where other flavourings predominate. If you wish to substitute stevia in other recipes, instead of the stewed dates which I have used as a sweetener, you will need to add some puréed apple, carrot or banana to take the place of the dried fruit, as well as ⅛–¼ teaspoon of stevia.

EGG REPLACERS

Egg replacers can be used to bind ingredients together but they will not help a mixture to rise. If using in cakes instead of eggs it is advisable to add a little extra baking powder. Egg replacers are readily available in health food shops.

BAKING POWDER

Baking powder is best bought from a health food shop where it can be found free from gluten and aluminium derivatives. Do not over eat baked products, as baking powder is high in sodium. They have been included so that some treats are available. Alternatively, try to find potassium baking powder. See the list of suppliers in the appendix if you have difficulty obtaining either product.

FLOURS FOR THICKENING

Corn flour (cornstarch) has been used as a thickening agent in some recipes. The corn flour (cornstarch) that I use can be bought in health food and whole food shops. It is very finely ground maize meal and is yellow in colour. The white cornflour (cornstarch) bought in supermarkets has been bleached.

Other flours can be substituted as a thickening agent but the amount used may need to be adjusted. To thicken 425ml/15fl oz/2 cups of liquid use one of the following:

15ml/1tbsp potato flour
30ml/2tbsp rice flour or unbleached corn flour (cornstarch)
45ml/3tbsp gram flour, soya flour

Cooking Terms

Sweating

Sweating is used in quite a few recipes to impart more flavour. This is not the same as sautéing or frying as the temperatures used are much lower. Heating oil to high temperatures is harmful because it starts to become toxic. Sweating involves softening the vegetables in oil, at a low temperature in an uncovered pan. The vegetables need to be stirred regularly with a wooden spoon until they begin to cook and brown. Sweating does take time, the amount of time being dependent on the type of vegetables. Allow approximately twenty minutes and sweat vegetables whilst you collect other ingredients together to save time.

Measuring Ingredients

For the best results when measuring teaspoons or tablespoons it is necessary to use a bought measuring utensil. The same applies with American cup measures.

SoupsSoupsSoupsSoupsSoupsSoup

Soups

Vegetable Stock

I like to make up substantial quantities of vegetable stock and freeze ready for use in soups and casseroles.

- 1 large onion
- 1 garlic clove
- 1 tbsp olive oil
- 2 medium carrots
- 3 celery stalks
- 1 medium potato
- 1 large tomato
- vegetable trimmings e.g. onion skins, celery tops, mushroom peelings, potato peelings, tomato skins etc.
- 3 dried porcini mushrooms
- 6 whole black peppercorns
- 1 bayleaf
- ½tsp dried thyme
- ½tsp dried rosemary
- bunch of parsley, including stems
- 2.75 litres/100fl oz/12 cups water
- salt

1. Dice the onion and crush the garlic clove. Place in a saucepan with the olive oil and sweat them in the oil until the onion begins to soften.
2. Dice the carrots, celery and potato and add to the pan. Continue to sweat the vegetables until they begin to brown.
3. Cut the tomato, vegetable trimmings and porcini mushrooms into small pieces. Add to the pan along with the peppercorns, bayleaf, thyme, rosemary and parsley.
4. Pour the water over the vegetables, bring to the boil and simmer for 1 hour.
5. Strain the stock and season lightly with salt. Store 2–3 days in the refrigerator or freeze in conveniently-sized containers.

Spicy Lentil and Aduki Bean Soup

Serves 4

This soup has lots of body and flavour – ideal for cold winter days.

- 60g/2oz/heaping ¼ cup aduki beans
- 1.5 litres/50fl oz/6¼ cups water *or* vegetable stock
- 1 large onion
- 1 large carrot
- 60g/2oz/⅓ cup sweetcorn
- 60g/2oz/heaping ¼ cup red split lentils
- 400g/14oz can chopped tomatoes
- 1tbsp chopped fresh basil
- 1tbsp chopped fresh coriander (cilantro)
- 1tbsp chopped fresh mint
- 1tbsp chopped fresh parsley
- 1 garlic clove
- 1cm/½in piece fresh ginger
- 1 small red or green chilli, deseeded *or* an extra 1cm/½in piece fresh ginger
- juice of 1 orange
- 2tsp lemon juice
- salt and freshly ground black pepper

1. Cook the beans in 600ml/20fl oz/2½ cups of water or stock until soft. This will take approximately 40–60 minutes, depending on the age of the beans. Soak the beans first to shorten the cooking time, if desired. After cooking there should be approximately 300ml/10fl oz/1¼ cups of cooking liquid remaining. Add more water, if necessary, to make it up to this amount.
2. Finely dice the onion and carrot and add to the beans along with the sweetcorn, lentils, chopped tomatoes and the remaining water or stock. Bring to the boil and simmer for approximately 20 minutes or until the lentils are soft.
3. Place the basil, coriander (cilantro), mint, parsley, garlic, ginger, chilli, orange juice and lemon juice in a food processor and process until smooth. If you do not have a food processor, chop everything as finely as possible and then mix with the orange and lemon juice.
4. Add the mixture to the soup. Bring to the boil, simmer for 2 minutes, then season to taste with salt and black pepper and serve.

Pumpkin and Carrot Soup

Serves 4

Pumpkins produce lovely soup. They break down when cooked to form a smooth, creamy textured purée, full of colour, and with a subtle flavour which allows you to taste the other ingredients.

1 large onion
1tbsp olive oil
450g/1lb pumpkin flesh
2 large carrots
3.5cm/1½ in piece fresh ginger
600ml/20fl oz/2½ cups vegetable stock
600ml/20fl oz/2½ cups water
1tsp ground cinnamon
1 large bayleaf
salt and freshly ground black pepper

1. Finely dice the onion and place in a saucepan with the olive oil. Sweat the onion in the oil until it begins to soften and brown.
2. Dice the pumpkin flesh (you do not need to remove the skin from the pumpkin provided it is not marked or tough) and slice the carrots.
3. Add the pumpkin and carrots to the pan and continue to sweat the vegetables until the pumpkin flesh starts to soften.
4. Grate the ginger and add to the pan along with the stock, water, cinnamon and bayleaf.
5. Bring to the boil and simmer until all the vegetables are tender. Remove the bayleaf.
6. Place the soup in a food processor and process until smooth. If you do not have a food processor mash the vegetables to break up the pumpkin.
7. Season to taste with salt and black pepper and serve.

Tuscan Bean and Cabbage Soup

Serves 4

Simple ingredients blend together in this soup to produce a hearty broth full of natural goodness.

1 large onion
350g/12oz white cabbage
1 large courgette (zucchini)
1 garlic clove
1tbsp olive oil
400g/14oz can butter, lima *or* cannellini beans
90g/3oz/¾ cup fresh *or* frozen peas
1.5 litres/50fl oz/6¼ cups good quality vegetable stock
½tsp dried rosemary
½tsp dried thyme
½tsp dried marjoram
1 bayleaf
2tbsp chopped fresh parsley
salt and freshly ground black pepper

1 Dice the onion, cabbage and courgette (zucchini), and crush the garlic clove.
2 Place the onion and garlic in a saucepan with the olive oil and sweat them in the oil for 5 minutes. Add the cabbage and courgette (zucchini) and continue to sweat the vegetables until they have all softened.
3 Drain the beans and add to the pan along with the peas, stock, rosemary, thyme, marjoram and bayleaf. Bring to the boil and simmer for 10 minutes.
4 Remove the bayleaf and add the parsley.
5 Season to taste with salt and black pepper and serve.

Spinach and Coconut Soup

Serves 4

This is quite a rich soup but delicious if served in small portions. Its light green colour makes it look most attractive when served.

1 large onion
2tsp olive oil
400g/14oz spinach
90g/3oz creamed coconut
300ml/10fl oz/1¼ cups vegetable stock
425ml/15fl oz/2 cups water
425ml/15fl oz/2 cups soya milk
½tsp grated nutmeg
salt and freshly ground black pepper

1. Finely dice the onion, place in a saucepan with the olive oil and sweat the onion in the oil until soft.
2. Add the spinach and sweat it until soft, approximately 2 minutes. Do not overcook or the spinach will lose its bright green colour.
3. Cut the creamed coconut into pieces, place in a food processor with the onion and spinach, and process. If you do not have a food processor, press the spinach and onion through a sieve and dissolve the creamed coconut in the stock or water.
4. Return to the pan and add the stock, water, soya milk and nutmeg.
5. Bring to the boil, season to taste with salt and black pepper and serve immediately.

Thai Rice Noodle Broth

Serves 4

Do make the effort to obtain the ingredients for this oriental soup, because it is so easy to make, yet the flavours when combined are truly wonderful. Kaffir lime leaves are available dried if you cannot find any fresh.

600ml/20fl oz/2½ cups vegetable stock
850ml/30fl oz/3¾ cups water
60g/2oz creamed coconut
2tsp lemon juice
½tsp grated lemon rind
2.5cm/1in piece fresh ginger, grated
1 garlic clove, crushed
2tsp tomato paste
2tsp Chinese five spice powder
2 kaffir lime leaves
60g/2oz thin rice noodles
1 bunch spring (green) onions
125g/4oz spinach
150g/5oz tofu
225g/8oz/2½ cups beansprouts
1tsp creamed basil *or* 1tbsp chopped fresh basil
1tbsp chopped fresh coriander (cilantro)
salt and freshly ground black pepper

1. Place the stock and water in a saucepan with the creamed coconut, lemon juice, lemon rind, ginger, garlic, tomato paste, Chinese five spice powder, kaffir lime leaves and rice noodles. Bring to the boil and simmer for 5 minutes.
2. Slice the spring (green) onions and spinach, and cube the tofu. Add these to the pan along with the beansprouts, basil and fresh coriander (cilantro). Bring to the boil and simmer for 3–5 minutes until the spinach and spring (green) onions are just cooked. Season to taste with salt and black pepper, remove the kaffir lime leaves and serve.

Sweetcorn and Potato Chowder

Serves 4

In this soup, potatoes and sweetcorn nestle in a creamy sauce that is subtly flavoured with herbs and spices. Substitute fresh sweetcorn, if available, to replace the canned or frozen, and add with the potatoes.

1 large onion
2tsp olive oil
½tsp grated nutmeg
1tsp cumin seeds
¼tsp dried sage
1 bayleaf
450g/1lb potatoes
425ml/15fl oz/2 cups vegetable stock
425ml/15fl oz/2 cups water
1tbsp rice flour
300ml/10fl oz/1¼ cups soya milk
326g/12oz can sweetcorn *or* 285g/10oz frozen sweetcorn
salt and freshly ground black pepper

1. Dice the onion, then place in a saucepan with the olive oil. Sweat the onion in the oil until it begins to soften and brown. Add the nutmeg, cumin seeds, sage and bayleaf, and sweat the ingredients for another 2 minutes.
2. Peel the potatoes and cut into 1cm/½ inch cubes. Add the potatoes, stock and water to the pan. Bring to the boil and simmer for 5–10 minutes or until the potatoes are just cooked but still holding their shape.
3. Mix the rice flour with the soya milk and add to the pan along with the sweetcorn.
4. Bring to the boil, stirring regularly, and simmer for 2 minutes. Season to taste with salt and black pepper, remove the bayleaf and serve.

Fresh Tomato, Mint and Pumpkin Soup

Serves 4

This is the ideal soup to make in autumn when there is a glut of fresh tomatoes, and pumpkins are just arriving in the shops. The flavours complement each other wonderfully well. Canned tomatoes could be used but the soup will loose some of its fresh tomato taste.

2 onions
2tsp olive oil
565g/1¼ lbs pumpkin flesh
600ml/20fl oz/2½ cups vegetable stock *or* water
565g/1¼ lbs fresh tomatoes
1 heaped tbsp tomato paste
1tbsp chopped fresh mint
1tbsp chopped fresh parsley
salt and freshly ground black pepper

1. Finely dice the onions and place in a saucepan with the olive oil. Sweat the onions in the oil until they begin to soften.
2. Dice the pumpkin flesh and add to the pan. Continue to sweat the vegetables until the pumpkin begins to soften. Add the stock or water, bring to the boil and simmer until the pumpkin is cooked.
3. Place the tomatoes in boiling water for 30 seconds to loosen the skins, then peel them. Place the pumpkin and onion mixture in a food processor with the peeled tomatoes, tomato paste and herbs, and process. If you do not have a food processor, mash the cooked pumpkin and onions, and finely dice the tomatoes before adding.
4. Return the ingredients to the pan and bring to the boil. Remove from the heat, season to taste with salt and black pepper and serve.

Lentil and Coconut Soup

Serves 4

The coconut makes this into a rich, creamy soup that is delicious served in small portions.

2 large onions
1 garlic clove
2tsp grated fresh ginger
1tbsp olive oil
1 heaped tsp ground coriander
1tsp ground cardamom
1tsp ground cinnamon
¼tsp ground cloves
175g/6oz/scant 1 cup red split lentils
600ml/20fl oz/2½ cups vegetable stock
90g/3oz creamed coconut
850ml/30fl oz/3¾ cups water
1tbsp tomato paste, optional
salt and freshly ground black pepper
fresh parsley, to garnish

1. Dice the onions and crush the garlic clove, then place in a saucepan with the ginger and olive oil. Sweat the onions, garlic and ginger in the oil until the onion begins to soften and brown.
2. Add the ground coriander, cardamom, cinnamon and cloves, and sweat the contents of the pan for a few more minutes.
3. Add the split lentils and stock, bring to the boil and simmer until the lentils are soft, approximately 20–25 minutes.
4. Place the soup in a food processor and process until smooth, or press through a sieve to purée most of the mixture.
5. Boil 300ml/10fl oz/1¼ cups of the water and dissolve the creamed coconut in it. Add to the soup along with the remaining water, tomato paste and salt and black pepper to taste.
6. Heat through and serve, garnished with chopped parsley.

Mung Bean and Coconut Soup

Substitute mung beans for the lentils in the above recipe but cook the beans for 40 minutes or until fairly soft before adding to the soup.

Leek and Spinach Soup

Serves 4

Nuts are a useful addition to soup as they produce rich creamy soup without the need to resort to dairy produce. If you do not have a food processor, use ground almonds instead of the cashews, and dice all the vegetables as finely as possible.

450g/1lb leeks
2 medium onions
225g/8oz spinach
2tsp olive oil
60g/2oz/scant ½ cup cashew nuts
300ml/10fl oz/1¼ cups soya milk
300ml/10fl oz/1¼ cups vegetable stock
600ml/20fl oz/2½ cups water
salt and freshly ground black pepper

1 Slice the leeks, dice the onions and cut spinach into pieces.
2 Place the leek and onion in a saucepan with the olive oil and sweat the vegetables in the oil until they are soft. Add the spinach and continue to sweat the vegetables until the spinach wilts, approximately 2 minutes. Do not overcook the spinach or it will lose its bright green colour.
3 Process the cashew nuts in a food processor until finely ground, then add the leek, spinach and onion mixture and the soya milk. Process again until smooth.
4 Pour the mixture back into the pan, add the stock and water, bring to the boil and simmer for 5 minutes. Season to taste with salt and black pepper and serve.

Continental Lentil and Mushroom Soup

Serves 4

This is one of my favourite soup recipes. It makes a really delicious, full-flavoured soup. Substitute leeks for the onions, if preferred.

10g/½oz dried porcini mushrooms
150ml/5fl oz/⅔ cup boiling water
1 large *or* 2 medium onions
2 garlic cloves
2tsp olive oil
225g/8oz field mushrooms
1.5 litres/50fl oz/6¼ cups vegetable stock
225g/8oz/heaping 1 cup continental lentils
½tsp dried thyme
½tsp dried rosemary
1 bayleaf
1tbsp tomato paste, optional
salt and freshly ground black pepper
1tbsp chopped fresh parsley

1 Soak the porcini mushrooms in the boiling water.
2 Finely dice the onions and crush the garlic cloves, and place in a saucepan with the olive oil. Sweat the onions and garlic in the oil until the onion begins to soften and brown. Dice the field mushrooms, add to the pan, and sweat the vegetables for a further 5 minutes.
3 Drain the porcini mushrooms, reserving the soaking water, and finely dice them. Add to the pan, along with the mushroom soaking water and the stock.
4 Add the lentils, herbs and tomato paste, if using, bring to the boil and simmer for approximately 1 hour or until the lentils are soft.
5 Remove the bayleaf and season to taste with salt and black pepper. Add the parsley and serve.

Aduki Bean and Chestnut Soup

Serves 4

This unusual soup is full of flavour and very warming for cold winter days. I have used canned aduki or red kidney beans instead of the dried beans when I've been in a hurry and the soup has still been a winner.

- 125g/4oz/heaping ½ cup aduki beans
- 850ml/30fl oz/3¾ cups water
- 600ml/20fl oz/2½ cups vegetable stock
- 1 large onion
- 2 celery stalks
- 1 large carrot
- 1 garlic clove
- 1tbsp olive oil
- 400g/14oz can chopped tomatoes
- 220g/7½ oz tinned chestnut purée
- 2 bayleaves
- 1tsp dried thyme
- salt and freshly ground black pepper
- chopped fresh parsley, to garnish

1. Soak the beans in hot water for at least 3 hours. Rinse and drain.
2. Place the beans in a large saucepan, add the water and stock, and cook until soft. This will take approximately 40 minutes. (If using a pressure cooker use 1.2 litres/40fl oz/5 cups of stock and water and cook for approximately 5 minutes.)
3. Finely dice the onion, celery and carrot and crush the garlic clove. Place in a saucepan with the olive oil and sweat the vegetables in the oil until softened.
4. Add the cooked beans and cooking liquid along with the tomatoes, chestnut purée and herbs. Bring to the boil and simmer for 20 minutes. Remove the bayleaves.
5. Season to taste with salt and black pepper and sprinkle with parsley before serving.

Leek, Fennel and Celeriac Soup

Serves 4

These ingredients have flavours that combine well and are enhanced by the herb seeds. If you do not want a creamy soup, substitute stock for the soya milk.

2 large *or* 3 medium leeks
1 fennel
½ large celeriac
1tbsp olive oil
1tsp fennel seeds
1tsp dill seeds
1tsp celery seeds
850ml/30fl oz/3¾ cups vegetable stock
300ml/10fl oz/1¼ cups soya milk
salt and freshly ground black pepper

1 Slice the leeks and fennel and cube the celeriac. Place in a saucepan with the olive oil and sweat the vegetables in the oil until they begin to soften and brown. Add the fennel, dill and celery seeds and cook for a few more minutes.
2 Add the vegetable stock, bring to the boil and simmer until the vegetables are cooked, approximately 10–15 minutes.
3 Place the soup in a food processor and process until smooth. If you do not have a food processor, mash the soup to break up the vegetables. Add the soya milk and season to taste with salt and black pepper. Bring to the boil and serve.

Celery and Celeriac Soup

Substitute 3–4 large celery stalks for the fennel in the above recipe and onions for the leeks, if preferred. Keep the remaining ingredients the same and follow the above method.

Spicy Tomato Soup

Serves 4

This quick and easy soup is made even simpler if you use a food processor to chop and grate the vegetables.

1 large onion
2 garlic cloves
1tbsp olive oil
1 large carrot
1 large courgette (zucchini)
1 medium potato
600ml/20fl oz/2½ cups passata (sieved tomatoes)
1 litre/35fl oz/4½ cups water *or* vegetable stock
1 heaped tsp paprika
¼–½tsp chilli powder, optional
1tsp dried oregano
2tbsp chopped fresh basil
1tbsp chopped fresh coriander (cilantro)
1tbsp chopped fresh parsley
salt and freshly ground black pepper

1. Dice the onion and crush the garlic cloves. Place in a saucepan with the olive oil and sweat them in the oil for a few minutes.
2. Grate the carrot, courgette (zucchini) and potato and add to the onions. Continue to sweat the vegetables, stirring occasionally, until they are beginning to soften and brown.
3. Add the passata, water or stock, paprika, chilli powder and oregano. Bring to the boil and simmer for 10–15 minutes or until the vegetables are all tender.
4. Add the fresh herbs and season to taste with salt and black pepper. Simmer for 2 minutes and serve.

Cream of Vegetable Soup

Serves 4

Soups have become so sophisticated over the years that sometimes I long for a good old-fashioned vegetable broth. Although this one does include a lot of herbs, they impart a wonderful flavour and the soup is so easy to make.

1 onion
1 leek
2 carrots
1 small parsnip
175g/6oz celeriac
225g/8oz white cabbage
1 medium potato
3 mushrooms, optional
4tsp olive oil
1.2 litres/40fl oz/5 cups vegetable stock *or* water
¼tsp fennel seeds
½tsp celery seeds
¼tsp dill seeds
1 bayleaf
¼tsp dried thyme
¼tsp dried rosemary
¼tsp dried basil
300ml/10fl oz/1¼ cups soya milk
salt and freshly ground black pepper

1. Cut all the vegetables into small pieces.
2. Place the vegetables in a saucepan with the olive oil and sweat them in the oil for approximately 20 minutes or until they begin to soften and brown. Stir regularly.
3. Add the stock or water and herbs, bring to the boil and simmer for 10 minutes or until the vegetables are just cooked.
4. Place one quarter of the soup in a food processor and process. Return it to the pan and add the soya milk. If you do not have a food processor, mash one quarter of the soup until smooth.
5. Heat through, season to taste with salt and black pepper, remove the bayleaf and serve.

Sweet Potato and Cauliflower Soup

Serves 4

Tarragon and chervil impart a lovely flavour to this soup, therefore disguising a frequently despised vegetable, the cauliflower. I find soups an ideal way to encourage children to eat vegetables.

1 onion
2tsp olive oil
350g/12oz sweet potato
450g/1lb cauliflower
600ml/20fl oz/2½ cups carrot juice
750ml/25fl oz/3 cups vegetable stock
1tbsp chopped fresh tarragon *or* 1tsp dried tarragon
1tbsp chopped fresh chervil *or* 1tsp dried chervil
salt and freshly ground black pepper
chopped fresh parsley, to garnish

1. Dice the onion and place in a saucepan with the olive oil. Sweat the onion in the oil until it begins to soften.
2. Dice the sweet potato flesh and break the cauliflower into florets. Add to the onion in the pan and sweat the vegetables for another 10 minutes or until the sweet potato and cauliflower are beginning to soften.
3. Add the carrot juice, bring to the boil and simmer until all the vegetables are just cooked.
4. Place in a food processor and process or mash until smooth.
5. Return the mixture to the pan and add the vegetable stock, tarragon and chervil.
6. Bring to the boil and simmer for a few minutes. Season to taste with salt and black pepper and serve garnished with parsley.

FirstCoursesFirstCoursesFirstCours

stCoursesFirstCourses

FirstCourses

Chilli Bean Pâté

Serves 4

For speed and convenience, I frequently use canned red kidney beans to make this pâté. I find pâtés useful for between-meal snacks and suppers, as well as first courses.

1 shallot
1cm/½in piece fresh ginger
1 garlic clove
1tsp olive oil
1tsp sesame oil
1tsp ground cumin
1tsp ground coriander
1tsp paprika
½tsp chilli powder
225g/8oz/heaping 1 cup cooked red kidney beans
salt and freshly ground black pepper

1 Finely dice the shallot, grate the ginger and crush the garlic clove. Place in a saucepan with the olive and sesame oil and sweat them until soft.
2 Add the cumin, ground coriander, paprika and chilli powder and sweat the ingredients for a few more minutes.
3 Place the onions and spice mixture in a food processor along with the drained red kidney beans. Process until smooth, adding a few tablespoons of water if necessary. If you do not have a food processor, mash well to break up and blend the ingredients.
4 Season with salt and black pepper and serve as a pâté with a small salad, as a spread for crisp-breads or rice cakes or as a filling for baked potatoes. This pâté can also be frozen.

Aubergine and Sun-Dried Tomato Pâté

Serves 4

If I have an aubergine (eggplant) to spare and the oven is on, I often cook the aubergine (eggplant) and store it in the refrigerator until needed. A small slice of bread can be used instead of the rice cakes in this recipe.

1 medium aubergine (eggplant)
1 large tomato
5 rice cakes
4 large sun-dried tomatoes
2tsp olive oil
1 heaped tbsp light tahini
1 heaped tsp chopped fresh chives
1 heaped tsp chopped fresh thyme
or ¼tsp each dried thyme and chives
salt and freshly ground black pepper

1. Wrap the aubergine (eggplant) in foil and bake in a moderate–hot oven for approximately 1 hour or until soft. Allow the aubergine (eggplant) to cool, then cut into chunks.
2. Place the tomato in boiling water for 30 seconds to loosen the skin, then peel.
3. Place the rice cakes in a food processor and process until they form fine crumbs. Add the aubergine (eggplant) chunks, tomato, sun-dried tomatoes, olive oil, tahini and fresh herbs and process until the pâté is smooth. Season to taste with salt and black pepper. If you do not have a food processor, crush the rice cakes in a plastic bag using a rolling pin, mash the aubergine (eggplant) and tomato until smooth, and finely dice the sun-dried tomatoes and herbs. Combine all the ingredients and mix well.
4. Serve the pâté in individual ramekin dishes (custard cups), accompanied by a salad garnish and rice cakes or wheat-free crispbreads. This pâté can be frozen.

Lentil Pâté

Serves 4

Served warm, this pâté can also be used as a filling for baked potatoes or taco shells.

- 125g/4 oz/heaping ½ cup red lentils
- 300ml/10fl oz/1¼ cups boiling water
- 90g/3oz onion
- 90g/3oz carrot
- 1 garlic clove
- 2tsp olive oil
- 1tsp ground cumin
- ½tsp turmeric
- ½tsp ground coriander
- salt and freshly ground black pepper

1. Place the lentils in a pan with the boiling water. Cover and simmer until the lentils are soft and the mixture starts to become a thick purée. This will take approximately 40 minutes.
2. Finely dice the onion, grate the carrot and crush the garlic clove. Place in a saucepan with the olive oil and sweat the vegetables in the oil until they are soft.
3. Add the cumin, turmeric and ground coriander and continue to cook for 1 minute.
4. Mix the lentils into the spicy onion mixture and season to taste with salt and black pepper. Allow the pâté to cool and serve in individual ramekin dishes (custard cups). Accompany with a salad garnish and rice cakes or wheat-free crackers. This pâté freezes well.

Humous and Grated Carrot Pâté

Serves 4–6

I use canned chick peas (garbanzo beans) as these are now readily available free from added salt and sugar. This delicious spread can also be used as a filling for baked potatoes or sandwiches.

225g/8oz carrots
225g/8oz/heaping 1 cup cooked chick peas (garbanzo beans)
2tbsp lemon juice
3 rounded tbsp light tahini
2 spring (green) onions
1tbsp olive oil
fresh herbs, to garnish

1 Finely grate the carrots.
2 Place the remaining ingredients, except the fresh herbs, in a food processor and process until a soft, smooth pâté is obtained. Use a little water if necessary to obtain the right consistency.
3 Combine the carrots with the humous pâté and mix well.
4 Divide the pâté between individual ramekin dishes (custard cups), garnish with fresh herbs and serve alongside a small salad. Accompany with rice cakes or wheat-free crackers.

Baked Avocados with Plum Sauce

Serves 4

This dish is so appetising and attractive that it is difficult to believe it is so quick and easy to prepare. It can be served cold if desired.

8 ripe plums
2 large avocados
4tsp French Dressing, page 88
fresh herbs to garnish e.g. mint, parsley, coriander (cilantro)

1 Place the plums in boiling water for 30 seconds to loosen the skins. Drain and peel. Remove the stones from the plums and chop the flesh finely.
2 Divide the plum flesh evenly between 4 small ovenproof serving dishes.
3 Peel, halve and stone (pit) the avocados and place each half, cut side down, on a plum base.
4 Bake in a preheated 200°C/400°F/gas mark 6 oven for 5 minutes or until the avocados are just warmed through.
5 Pour 1 teaspoon of French dressing over each avocado and garnish with fresh herbs. Serve at once.

Roasted Red Peppers and Fennel with Pine Nuts and Olives

Serves 4

A wonderful combination of textures and flavours make this one of my favourite first courses, yet it is so easy to prepare.

2 large sweet red peppers
1 large fennel
3tbsp olive oil
1tbsp lemon juice, optional
salt and freshly ground black pepper
30g/1oz/¼ cup pine nuts
20 black olives
fresh herbs, to garnish

1. Quarter the sweet peppers and deseed. Remove any shoots from the fennel and cut the bulb in half. Cut each half into four segments, each containing a piece of the central core.
2. Place the sweet pepper and fennel segments on a greased baking tray.
3. Mix the olive oil and lemon juice, if using, and season with salt and black pepper. Brush the sweet peppers and fennel with this mixture.
4. Bake the vegetables in a preheated 200°C/400°F/gas mark 6 oven for approximately 20 minutes or until the vegetables are just cooked and starting to brown.
5. Toast the pine nuts in the oven for a few minutes.
6. Serve the peppers and fennel on individual plates, garnished with the black olives, toasted pine nuts and some fresh herbs. Can be served warm or cold.

Fresh Pears with Tomato French Dressing

Serves 4

This is another simple first course whose flavour, texture and colour belie its simple ingredients and ease of preparation.

2 large *or* 4 small ripe pears	Tomato French Dressing, page 89
¼ lettuce	fresh herbs to garnish e.g.
small bunch of watercress	parsley, chives, mint, dill,
2 tomatoes	tarragon

1 Peel, halve and core the pears.
2 Shred the lettuce and divide between 4 serving plates. Remove the stems from the watercress and scatter the leaves over the lettuce.
3 Place the tomatoes in boiling water for 30 seconds, then drain and peel off the skin. Cut the flesh into small dice (you could use the leftover tomato shells from the tomato French dressing). Sprinkle the diced tomato over the lettuce on each plate.
4 Place one or two upturned pears on each bed of lettuce.
5 Just before serving, pour 2 tablespoons of tomato French dressing over the pear or pears on each plate. Finely chop the fresh herbs, sprinkle over the pears and serve.

Vegetable Pancakes with Coriander, Mint and Red Chilli Sauce

Serves 4

Plain soya yogurt with no added sugar is now available in some health food shops (see back of book for list of suppliers). Other vegetables, such as mushrooms, spinach, sweetcorn, sweet peppers or cooked beans, can be mixed into the pancake batter.

1 small carrot
1 small courgette (zucchini)
4 spring (green) onions
60g/2oz/½ cup peas

PANCAKE BATTER
1 egg
1tsp baking powder
2tsp olive oil
125g/4oz/¾ cup plus 2tbsp rice flour
60ml/2fl oz/¼ cup water
90ml/3fl oz/⅓ cup soya milk
salt and freshly ground black pepper
olive oil for frying

CORIANDER, MINT AND CHILLI SAUCE
1 small red onion
½–1 red chilli
300ml/10fl oz/1¼ cups plain soya yogurt
1tbsp chopped fresh mint
1tbsp chopped fresh coriander (cilantro)

1. Grate the carrot on a fine grater and the courgette (zucchini) on a medium grater. Finely slice the spring (green) onions.
2. To make the pancake batter, place all ingredients in a food processor and process until blended. If you do not have a food processor, beat the egg and combine with the remaining ingredients.
3. Mix the vegetables into the pancake batter and place tablespoons of the mixture into a greased frying pan or griddle. Cook until brown, then turn and cook the other side.
4. Meanwhile, make the sauce. Very finely dice the onion, and deseed and dice the chilli. Combine the onion and chilli with the yogurt, mint and coriander (cilantro).
5. Serve 2–3 pancakes per person, accompanied by the sauce.

Carrot and Avocado Terrine

Serves 4–6

This delightful dish is colourful and stylish, and would grace any dinner party table. It has a subtle blend of flavours and a rich creamy texture.

CARROT LAYER
350g/12oz carrots
125g/4oz/1⅓ cups ground almonds
1tsp chopped fresh mint
1tbsp chopped fresh chives
salt and freshly ground black pepper

AVOCADO LAYER
1 large avocado
90g/3oz/1 cup ground almonds
2tsp lemon juice
salt and freshly ground black pepper

sliced oranges and watercress, to garnish

1 Slice the carrots and cook until tender. Drain and cool.
2 Place the carrots in a food processor and process until fairly smooth. Add the ground almonds, mint, chives, salt and black pepper and process again. You will have to use a spatula to scrape the sides of the bowl at intervals, as the mixture will be quite stiff. If you do not have a food processor, mash the carrots, finely dice the mint and chives and then combine them all.
3 Layer half the carrot mixture in a lined 450g/1lb loaf tin (pan) and reserve the second half until later.
4 Place the avocado in a food processor and process until smooth. Add the ground almonds, lemon juice and salt and black pepper and process again. If you do not have a food processor, mash the avocado, then combine with the remaining ingredients.
5 Layer the avocado mixture on top of the carrot mixture in the loaf tin (pan). Place the reserved carrot mixture on top and level the surface. Place the terrine in the refrigerator to cool for at least 1 hour.
6 Turn the terrine out on to a plate and remove the lining paper. Garnish with sliced oranges and watercress. Serve cut into slices and accompany with rice cakes or wheat-free crackers if desired.

Spiced Potato Cakes with Mint and Yogurt Dip

Serves 4

Plain soya yogurt free from added sugar is now available in many health food shops (see index for list of suppliers). The potato cakes can be made in quantity and frozen ready for future use.

POTATO CAKES
680g/1½lbs potatoes
1 medium onion
2tsp olive oil
1 heaped tsp ground coriander
1 heaped tsp ground cumin
½tsp turmeric
15g/½oz/1tbsp margarine
2 rounded tbsp rice flour
salt and freshly ground black pepper
olive oil for frying
fresh mint, to garnish

MINT AND YOGURT DIP
300ml/10fl oz/1¼ cups soya yogurt
2tbsp chopped fresh mint
1tsp lemon juice, optional
freshly ground black pepper

1. First, make the mint and yogurt dip. Combine the soya yogurt with the chopped mint. The lemon juice will not be needed if the yogurt is quite tart, so only add if required. Season with black pepper and allow the dip to stand for the flavours to combine.
2. Cook the potatoes until tender.
3. Finely dice the onion, place in a saucepan with the olive oil and sweat the onion in the oil until soft. Add the spices and continue to sweat the ingredients for a few more minutes.
4. Mash the potatoes until smooth. Add the margarine, the onion and spice mixture, the rice flour, salt and black pepper. Mix to combine.
5. Divide the mixture into 10 portions. Using floured hands form each portion into a flattened cake approximately 1cm/½ inch thick.
6. Fry the potato cakes in a little oil until golden brown on each side.
7. Serve two potato cakes on each plate with a little mint and yogurt dip and a garnish of mint leaves. The potato cakes can be frozen.

Celeriac and Potato Rosti

Serves 4

If desired, make individual rosti by pressing the mixture into a metal pastry cutter placed in the frying pan. Make each cake approximately 1cm/½ inch thick and press the mixture down to form a round before removing the cutter.

350g/12oz peeled potatoes
350g/12oz peeled celeriac
2tbsp olive oil
15g/½oz/1tbsp margarine
½tsp grated nutmeg
salt and freshly ground black pepper

1. Cut the potatoes and celeriac into large pieces, cover with boiling water and boil for 5 minutes. Drain.
2. Grate the potatoes and celeriac on a large-holed grater.
3. Place the potatoes and celeriac in a large saucepan, add 1 tablespoon of the olive oil and sweat the vegetables in the oil, stirring frequently, until they are starting to brown but are not cooked.
4. Add the margarine, nutmeg, salt and black pepper and mix well.
5. Grease a medium-sized frying pan with olive oil, add the potato mixture and press it into a large pancake.
6. Cook the rosti on a medium heat until the underside is brown, approximately 10 minutes.
7. Slide the mixture out of the pan on to a chopping board, cooked side downwards. Grease the pan with the remaining oil and invert the pan over the rosti. Lift both the pan and the chopping board and turn over so that the mixture tips into the frying pan with the uncooked side downwards.
8. Cook for another 10 minutes or until the underside is brown. Cut into wedges and serve with a salad garnish.

Oven-Baked Spanish Tortilla

Serves 4

A tortilla is like an oven-baked omelette, but packed full of succulent vegetables. It makes a substantial main course for two people served with salads and potatoes.

450g/1lb selection of vegetables e.g. sweet peppers, mushrooms, onions, courgettes (zucchini), broccoli, peas, sweetcorn
1tbsp olive oil
4 eggs
200ml/7fl oz/¾ cup soya milk
2tbsp rice flour
salt and freshly ground black pepper
1 large tomato
8 black olives

1 Cut the vegetables into shapes that will cook in approximately the same amount of time.
2 Place the vegetables in a saucepan with the olive oil and sweat them in the oil until they begin to soften and brown. If using vegetables which take longer to cook, start with these first.
3 Beat the eggs with the soya milk and rice flour, then season with salt and black pepper.
4 Place the vegetables in a greased 20cm/8 inch flan dish and pour the egg mixture over the top.
5 Slice the tomato and place the slices on top of the tortilla along with the black olives.
6 Bake in a preheated 170°C/325°F/gas mark 3 oven for approximately 30 minutes or until the tortilla is just set and beginning to brown. Cut into wedges and serve with a salad garnish.

Stuffed Aubergine Slices with Tomato and Chilli

Serves 4

A spicy dish of succulent aubergines (eggplants) – full of flavour and delicious served hot or cold.

2 medium aubergines (eggplants)
1 onion
2 garlic cloves
1 green chilli
2tsp olive oil
10 sun-dried tomatoes
1 large tomato
20 olives
1tsp dried basil
1tsp dried oregano
125ml/4fl oz/½ cup tomato paste
freshly ground black pepper
cocktail sticks (toothpicks)
extra olive oil
chopped fresh herbs, to garnish

1 Cut each aubergine (eggplant) lengthways into 1cm/½ inch slices, if possible cutting each into 8 slices so that you have 6 middle slices, and 2 end slices to add to the filling.
2 Finely dice the onion and the 4 aubergine (eggplant) end slices. Crush the garlic cloves. Deseed and finely dice the green chilli.
3 Place the onion, diced aubergine (eggplant), garlic and chilli in a saucepan with the olive oil and sweat the vegetables in the oil until they soften and begin to brown.
4 Finely dice the sun-dried tomatoes and fresh tomato and quarter the olives. Add to the pan along with the herbs, tomato paste and black pepper. Mix well.
5 Brush one side of each aubergine (eggplant) slice with olive oil, turn the slices over and divide the stuffing mixture between the slices. Spread the mixture along the length of the slices, leaving 2.5cm/1 inch at the wide end empty.
6 Roll each aubergine (eggplant) slice, starting at the narrowest end and with the stuffing mixture on the inside. If the aubergines (eggplants) will not roll well because they are too fresh and stiff, leave

for 30 minutes in the heat of the kitchen and they will soften a little. Secure each aubergine (eggplant) roll with a cocktail stick (toothpick).

7 Place the aubergine (eggplant) rolls in a baking dish and drizzle the surface of each with olive oil. Add 60ml/2fl oz/¼ cup of water to the dish and cover with foil.

8 Bake in a preheated 200°C/400°F/gas mark 6 oven for approximately 40 minutes or until the aubergines (eggplants) are soft and well cooked. Garnish with fresh herbs and serve.

Nut-Stuffed Mushrooms

Serves 4

There is a lovely contrast between the crispy nut filling and the moist texture of the mushrooms in this recipe.

- 2–3 large field mushrooms per person (plus 1 extra)
- 1 large onion
- 2 garlic cloves
- 2tsp olive oil
- 60g/2oz/scant ½ cup hazelnuts
- 15g/½oz/1tbsp margarine
- ½tsp dried thyme
- ½tsp dried rosemary
- 1tbsp chopped fresh herbs e.g. parsley, fennel, dill, chives
- salt and freshly ground black pepper

1. Cut the stems from the mushrooms and finely dice these along with one whole mushroom.
2. Finely dice the onion and crush the garlic cloves.
3. Place the onion and garlic in a saucepan with the olive oil and sweat them in the oil until the onion is soft and beginning to brown. Add the chopped mushroom stalks and sweat the vegetables for a few more minutes.
4. Lightly toast the hazelnuts in a medium oven or grill (broiler) and remove the skins.
5. Grind the hazelnuts fairly finely in a food processor or using a mortar and pestle and add to the pan along with the margarine, dried herbs, fresh herbs and salt and black pepper to taste. Mix to combine.
6. Place the field mushrooms, stem side up, on a baking tray. Divide the mixture between the mushrooms and spread over the surface of each one.
7. Bake in a preheated 200°C/400°F/gas mark 6 oven for 5–8 minutes or until the tops are beginning to brown and the mushrooms are just cooked. Serve 2–3 mushrooms on each plate along with a salad garnish.

Stuffed Tomatoes

Serves 4

This is a delightful recipe – succulent tomatoes stuffed with a lentil and nut mixture, flavoured with herbs, and served hot from the oven.

- 4 large tomatoes
- 1 small onion
- 90g/3oz/scant ½ cup split red lentils
- 1 small bayleaf
- 60g/2oz/scant ½ cup hazelnuts
- 2tbsp mixed chopped fresh herbs e.g. parsley, mint, fennel, coriander (cilantro), basil, tarragon, thyme *or* 1tsp mixed dried herbs
- 2tsp tomato paste
- salt and freshly ground black pepper
- 2tsp sesame seeds
- lettuce and watercress, to garnish
- 1tbsp French Dressing, page 88

1 Cut the tomatoes in half from side to side rather than down through the stalk. Using a teaspoon, scoop out the centres. Finely chop the tomato pulp and place in a measuring jug with any juices. Make up to 350ml/12fl oz/1½ cups with water and place in a pan.

2 Finely chop the onion and add to the pan along with the lentils and bayleaf. Bring to the boil, cover and simmer for approximately 20 minutes or until the lentils are soft.

3 Remove the lid and continue to cook until all the liquid has been absorbed and the lentil mixture is fairly thick. Remove the bayleaf.

4 Toast the hazelnuts in a medium oven or grill (broiler) and finely chop. Add to the lentil mixture along with the chopped herbs and tomato paste. Season to taste with salt and black pepper. Mix well.

5 Pile the lentil mixture into the tomato shells and sprinkle the surface of each with sesame seeds. Place on a baking tray.

6 Bake in a preheated 200°C/400°F/gas mark 6 oven for 5–10 minutes until hot but not over cooked.

7 Meanwhile, shred the lettuce and watercress and toss in the dressing. Serve the tomatoes warm on a bed of dressed salad.

Felafel with Sweet and Sour Sauce

Serves 4

Once you have tasted this traditional Middle Eastern dish you will want to make it again and again. Canned chick peas (garbanzo beans) could be used as these are now readily available free from added salt and sugar – you will need 450g/1lb/heaping 2 cups to equate with the dried peas (beans).

225g/8oz/heaping 1 cup chick peas (garbanzo beans)
1 garlic clove
1tsp ground cumin
1tsp turmeric
½tsp chilli powder
3tbsp fresh or frozen coriander (cilantro)
3tbsp light tahini
75ml/2½fl oz/⅓ cup water
salt and freshly ground black pepper
rice flour for coating
olive oil for brushing

SWEET AND SOUR SAUCE
2 medium onions
5cm/2in piece fresh ginger
1tbsp olive oil
125g/4oz/⅔ cup chopped dates
350ml/12fl oz/1½ cups water
2tbsp lemon juice
2tsp mustard
2tbsp tomato paste
salt and freshly ground black pepper

1 Soak the chick peas (garbanzo beans) overnight in cold water. Drain, rinse and cook in lots of boiling water until the chick peas (garbanzo beans) are just cooked but not too soft, approximately 45–60 minutes. If using a pressure cooker this will only take about 3 minutes. Drain the chick peas (garbanzo beans).
2 Crush the garlic clove and place in a food processor with the chick peas (garbanzo beans), cumin, turmeric, chilli powder and fresh coriander (cilantro). Process until the chick peas (garbanzo beans) are finely chopped but not puréed. If you do not have a processor, mash the chick peas (garbanzo beans) with the spices.

3. Remove half the mixture and place in a bowl. Process the remaining half with the tahini and water until the mixture is smooth and creamy.
4. Combine the two mixtures and season to taste with salt and black pepper.
5. With floured hands, roll the mixture into 16 walnut-sized balls and place on a well-greased baking tray. Brush the surface of each felafel with olive oil and bake in a preheated 200°C/400°F/gas mark 6 oven for 15–20 minutes or until they begin to brown. Turn if necessary during cooking. Do not overcook the felafels or they will be too dry. Alternatively, the felafels could be fried.
6. While the felafels are cooking, prepare the sauce. Finely dice the onions and ginger, place in a saucepan with the olive oil and sweat them in the oil until the onion is beginning to soften and brown.
7. Add the chopped dates and water, bring to the boil and simmer for 5–10 minutes or until the dates are soft.
8. Add the lemon juice, mustard, tomato paste, salt and black pepper, and mix well. Place in a food processor and process to produce a smooth sauce. If you do not have a food processor, chop the onion very finely and grate the ginger, then beat the sauce well to make it as smooth as possible.
9. Serve the felafels hot with the sweet and sour sauce. The felafels and the sauce are both suitable for freezing.

Spiced Potato Wedges with Garlic Mayonnaise Dip

Serves 4

These potato wedges are also delicious served with Coriander, Mint and Chilli Sauce (page 73). The warm, crispy, spiced wedges contrast wonderfully with cool, moist sauces.

4 medium baking potatoes (approximately 900g/2lb in weight)
1tbsp lemon juice
2tbsp olive oil
½tsp chilli powder
salt and freshly ground black pepper
Garlic Mayonnaise, page 90
chopped fresh herbs, to garnish

1 Scrub the potatoes well. You do not need to peel them unless the skins are marked.
2 Cut the potatoes in half lengthways, then cut each half into four wedges lengthways. Dry the potato wedges on a tea towel.
3 In a large bowl, mix together the lemon juice, olive oil and chilli powder and season with salt and black pepper.
4 Toss the potato wedges in the oil mixture until well coated.
5 Place the potato wedges on a large baking tray and bake in a preheated 200°C/400°F/gas mark 6 oven for approximately 40 minutes or until brown and crisp on the outside and soft inside.
6 Divide the wedges between the serving plates and place a small dish of garlic mayonnaise on each. Garnish with fresh herbs.

Polenta with Fresh Tomato and Basil Sauce

Serves 4

Polenta is coarsely ground maize meal. The cooked polenta can be frozen once cut into rounds, then cooked on a griddle from frozen. It is also nice served with Coriander, Mint and Chilli Sauce (page 73).

POLENTA	TOMATO AND BASIL SAUCE
175g/6oz/1 cup plus 3tbsp polenta flour	3 ripe tomatoes
300ml/10fl oz/1¼ cups cold water	30g/1oz basil leaves
600ml/20fl oz/2½ cups boiling water	2 garlic cloves
30g/1oz/2tbsp margarine	3tbsp good quality olive oil
salt and freshly ground black pepper	salt and freshly ground black pepper

1 Place the polenta flour in a saucepan with the cold water and mix. Add the boiling water and bring to the boil, stirring constantly. Continue to cook the polenta over a low heat, stirring regularly, for approximately 5 minutes or until the mixture starts to come away from the sides of the pan.
2 Stir in the margarine and season with salt and black pepper.
3 Tip the polenta on to a work surface and press out until 1cm/½ inch thick. Allow the mixture to cool.
4 Cut the polenta into 10–12 rounds using a pastry cutter.
5 Place the polenta rounds onto a greased griddle or frying pan and cook until brown on both sides.
6 Meanwhile, prepare the sauce. Place the tomatoes in boiling water for 30 seconds, drain and peel them. Place the tomatoes, basil leaves, garlic and olive oil in a food processor and process until smooth. If you do not have a processor, finely chop the tomatoes and basil leaves and crush the garlic cloves. Mix the ingredients together.
7 Season the sauce and serve with the polenta.

SaladsSaladsSaladsSaladsSaladsSa

sSaladsSaladsSaladsSalads

Salads

French Dressing

If allowed, 1 teaspoon of honey makes this dressing taste less sharp. Alternatively, you could use an ⅛ teaspoon of stevia (see page 43). If you cannot tolerate citrus fruits but can tolerate cider vinegar, use one-third vinegar to two-thirds olive oil. Even nicer is a combination of cider vinegar and balsamic vinegar.

½tsp orange rind
½tsp lemon rind
juice of 1 orange
juice of 1 lemon
good quality olive oil
2tsp mustard
salt and freshly ground black pepper

2tsp mixed dried herbs e.g. dill, fennel seeds, celery seeds, tarragon, parsley, mint
or 2tbsp mixed chopped fresh herbs e.g. parsley, chives, tarragon, mint

1. Place the orange and lemon rind and orange and lemon juice in a screw-top jar, and add an equal amount of olive oil.
2. Add the remaining ingredients and shake well.
3. Store in the refrigerator, ready for use.

Tomato French Dressing

This recipe makes a delightful dressing. If the tomatoes are not very ripe you may need to use more than four. The leftover shells can be used in a salad or soup.

4 large very ripe tomatoes
1 garlic clove
100ml/3½fl oz/scant ½ cup good quality olive oil
1tbsp lemon juice
salt and freshly ground black pepper

1 Cut each tomato in half and scoop out the seeds, juice and fibres.
2 Crush the garlic clove and mix with the tomato pulp.
3 Press the tomato pulp and garlic through a sieve, using the back of a spoon, to remove the seeds and fibres. Measure the juice and if it does not make up 200ml/7fl oz/¾ cup, make it up to this amount using extra tomatoes.
4 Whisk the tomato juice with the olive oil and lemon juice. Season to taste with salt and black pepper. Store in the refrigerator and use within 7 days.

Tahini and Orange Salad Dressing

4tbsp light tahini
4tbsp water
2tbsp sunflower oil
180ml/6fl oz/scant ¾ cup orange juice
2tsp finely grated fresh ginger

1 Mix together the tahini and water until well blended.
2 Add the remaining ingredients and whisk the dressing until smooth.

Garlic Mayonnaise

This is a lovely light mayonnaise similar to the aioli served with crusty bread in Spanish restaurants.

2–3 garlic cloves 290g/10oz packet silken tofu 180ml/6fl oz/scant ¾ cup sunflower oil	salt and freshly ground black pepper

1 Crush the garlic cloves and process with the tofu until smooth.
2 Gradually add the sunflower oil with the food processor on full power until the ingredients are well combined. If you do not have a processor, beat the oil gradually into the tofu and garlic. Season with salt and black pepper. Refrigerate and use within 3 days.

Gomasio

Gomasio is a condiment made from roasted ground sesame seeds mixed with salt. It is delicious sprinkled over plain salads, especially if a good quality olive oil is drizzled over first.

20tsp sesame seeds	1tsp sea salt

1 Place the sesame seeds in a frying pan with the sea salt and dry roast over a moderate heat for a few minutes, stirring constantly, until the sesame seeds turn a slightly deeper brown and smell toasted. Alternatively, the seeds can be roasted in the oven.
2 Place the toasted seeds and salt in a food processor or mortar and pestle and grind until the seeds are partly broken down and powdery. Store in an airtight container.

Spinach, Pine Nut and Avocado Salad

Serves 4

This is one of my favourite salad recipes. It produces a salad with a delightful contrast of colours, textures and flavours.

60g/2oz small spinach leaves
60g/2oz lambs lettuce (mâche) *or* rocket leaves (arugula)
3 spring (green) onions
1 large avocado
16 cherry tomatoes
30g/1oz/heaping ¼ cup pine nuts
3tbsp French Dressing, page 88

1. Place the spinach leaves and lambs lettuce (mâche) or rocket (arugula) in a bowl.
2. Finely slice the spring (green) onions, cube the avocado and halve the cherry tomatoes. Add to the salad bowl.
3. Toast the pine nuts in a medium oven or grill (broiler) and add to the bowl.
4. Toss the salad with the French dressing and serve.

Peach, Broad Bean and Mangetout Salad

Serves 4

A wonderful combination of colours, textures and flavours make this a very appealing salad. I have not included a dressing with this salad but it is delicious served with Tomato French Dressing (page 89)

450g/1lb/2½ cups broad (fava) beans	¼ lettuce, i.e. cos, iceberg, frisee, curly endive
90g/3oz mangetout (snowpeas)	½ bunch watercress
2 peaches	

1 Shell the broad (fava) beans and cook in boiling water until tender, approximately 5 minutes. Allow to cool, then remove the skin from each bean by pressing between the fingers and thumb.
2 Blanch the mangetout (snowpeas) in boiling water for 1 minute. Allow them to cool.
3 Halve and stone (pit) each peach and cut into segments.
4 Shred the lettuce and remove any tough stems from the watercress.
5 Arrange the lettuce and watercress in a serving bowl, then arrange the broad (fava) beans, peaches and mangetout (snowpeas) on top. Serve the salad accompanied by tomato French dressing if desired.

Spinach & Coconut Soup (page 52) *with* Savoury Herb Scones (page 210)

Pumpkin & Carrot Soup (page 50)
***with* Tofu & Vegetable Kebabs with**
Oriental Pesto Sauce (page 155)

Apricot, Carrot & Polenta Cake (page 192) ***with*** **Caribbean Cobbler (pages 178 and 179)**

Vegetable Hotpot (page 118)
***with* Spinach, Pine Nut &**
Avocado Salad (page 91)

Creamy Cashew Nut & Almond Roast (pages 128 and 129) ***with*** **Peach, Broad Bean & Mangetout Salad (page 92)**

Leek & Potato Pie (page 157) ***with*** **Aduki Bean & Red Cabbage Casserole (pages 122 and 123)**

Roasted Red Peppers with Fennel, Pine Nuts & Olives (page 71) *with* Spiced Potato Wedges with Garlic Mayonnaise Dip (page 84)

Prune & Almond Tart (pages 166 and 177) *with* Hazelnut & Strawberry Tortes (page 174)

Tropical Rice Salad

Serves 4

The combination of savoury and sweet in this recipe works exceptionally well to produce an interesting, delicious and filling salad.

225g/8oz/1⅓ cups cooked rice
1 banana
1 medium orange
60g/2oz/½ cup pistachio nuts
90g/3oz/scant ½ cup sweetcorn

DRESSING
1tsp grated orange rind
4tbsp orange juice
2tbsp olive oil
1tsp mustard
1tbsp chopped fresh herbs e.g. mint, chives, dill, fennel, parsley

1. Place the cooked rice in a large bowl.
2. Peel the banana and cut into fine dice.
3. Grate the rind for the dressing from the orange, then remove the orange skin and cut the flesh into fine dice.
4. Mix the diced orange and banana into the rice along with the pistachio nuts and sweetcorn.
5. Whisk together the dressing ingredients and pour over the rice salad. Mix well and serve.

Julienne Salad

Serves 4

This is a quick, easy and colourful salad. I have not included a dressing with the salad but it goes well with Tahini and Orange Dressing or Tomato French Dressing (see index).

½ large cucumber
½ sweet green pepper
½ sweet red pepper
125g/4oz/heaping ½ cup sweetcorn
125g/4oz/1⅓ cups beansprouts
1tbsp chopped fresh parsley
freshly ground black pepper

1 Peel the cucumber, cut lengthways into two and scoop out the soft centre. Cut the flesh into julienne strips approximately 1 x 6cm/½ x 2½ inches.
2 Cut the sweet pepper halves into similar-sized julienne strips.
3 Combine the cucumber, sweet pepper, sweetcorn, beansprouts and parsley. Season with black pepper and serve.

Lentil and Tomato Salad

Serves 4

This salad is a combination of simple ingredients, skilfully put together to make a delicious dish.

125g/4oz/heaping ½ cup green lentils
850ml/30fl oz/3¾ cups boiling water
1 small bayleaf
3tbsp French Dressing, page 88
2 large tomatoes
½ small sweet red pepper
3 spring (green) onions
8 black olives
2tbsp chopped fresh parsley

1. Place the lentils in a pan with the boiling water and bayleaf. Bring to the boil and simmer until the lentils are cooked but not breaking up, approximately 30 minutes.
2. Drain the lentils, remove the bayleaf and place the lentils in a bowl. Stir in the French dressing while the lentils are still warm, then allow the lentils to cool.
3. Place the tomatoes in boiling water for 30 seconds to loosen the skins, then peel. Finely chop the tomato flesh and dice the sweet pepper. Slice the spring (green) onions and halve the black olives.
4. Add the tomatoes, sweet pepper, spring (green) onions and black olives to the cooled lentils along with the parsley. Mix well. Leave the salad to stand for at least 1 hour before serving, to allow the flavours to combine.

Celeriac, Carrot and Raisin Salad

Serves 4

75ml/2½fl oz/⅓ cup orange juice
1tbsp lemon juice
3tbsp olive oil
freshly ground black pepper
175g/6oz celeriac
175g/6oz carrots
60g/2oz/scant ½ cup raisins
30g/1oz/¼ cup toasted coconut chips

1 Mix together the orange juice, lemon juice, olive oil and black pepper in a bowl.
2 Grate the celeriac and carrots and add to the dressing, mixing well.
3 Add the raisins and leave the salad to soften for 1–2 hours, stirring occasionally.
4 Add the toasted coconut chips, mix and serve.

Potato and Cauliflower Salad

Serves 4

225g/8oz new potatoes
450g/1lb cauliflower florets
½ quantity of Garlic Mayonnaise, page 90
2tbsp chopped fresh tarragon
2tsp caraway seeds

1 Cover the potatoes with boiling water, cook until just tender and allow to cool.
2 Cover the cauliflower florets with boiling water and simmer until lightly cooked but still retaining a little crispness. Allow to cool.
3 Dice the potatoes and combine with the cauliflower florets, garlic mayonnaise, chopped tarragon and caraway seeds. Leave the salad to stand for 1 hour before serving, to allow the flavours to combine.

Pasta Salad

Serves 4

The advent of wheat-free pasta means that old favourites such as pasta salad can be enjoyed. This vegetarian version is full of flavour, colour and texture; a must for any salad.

225g/8oz wheat-free pasta spirals
90ml/3fl oz/⅓ cup French Dressing, page 88
½ small sweet red pepper
4 sun-dried tomatoes
3 spring (green) onions
12 black olives
8 cherry tomatoes
30g/1oz/heaping ¼ cup pine nuts
1tbsp chopped fresh herbs e.g. parsley, fennel, dill, basil, chives, tarragon

1 Cook the pasta according to the instructions or until just soft. Drain the pasta and place in a bowl. Add the French dressing while the pasta is still warm, and toss to coat the pasta with the dressing. Allow the pasta to cool.
2 Finely dice the sweet pepper and sun-dried tomatoes. Finely slice the spring (green) onions and halve the olives and cherry tomatoes.
3 Toast the pine nuts in a medium oven or grill (broiler) and add to the pasta along with all the other ingredients. Gently mix together and leave the salad to stand for 1 hour before serving, to allow the flavours to combine.

Roasted Courgette Salad

Serves 4

In this recipe, the soft texture and colour of roasted vegetables is contrasted by crunchy nuts, juicy red tomatoes and succulent black olives.

12 small courgettes (zucchini)
2 garlic cloves
1tbsp olive oil
10 cherry tomatoes
8 olives
15g/½oz/2tbsp pine nuts
2–3tbsp French Dressing, page 88 *or* Tomato French Dressing, page 89

1 Cut the courgettes (zucchini) into 1.5cm/¾ inch lengths and place in a bowl.
2 Crush the garlic cloves and add to the bowl along with the olive oil. Toss the courgette (zucchini) slices until evenly coated with the olive oil and garlic.
3 Place the courgette (zucchini) slices on a greased baking tray and bake in a preheated 200°C/400°F/gas mark 6 oven for approximately 15 minutes or until browning and lightly cooked but not too soft. Allow the courgettes (zucchini) to cool.
4 Place the courgettes (zucchini) in a bowl. Halve the cherry tomatoes and olives and add to the bowl. Toast the pine nuts in a medium oven or grill (broiler) and add along with the dressing. Mix well and serve.

Roasted Sweet Pepper Salad with Lemon and Mint

Serves 4

This is a luscious dish in which lemon pieces are cooked and then added to the salad ingredients, producing a burst of flavour. Lemons preserved in brine could be used instead, if these are available. Although there seems to be lots of sweet peppers in this recipe they do become less bulky when cooked.

2 sweet green peppers
2 sweet red peppers
2 sweet yellow peppers
olive oil for brushing
1 large lemon
2tbsp chopped fresh mint
4tbsp good quality olive oil
freshly ground black pepper

1 Halve and deseed the sweet peppers and place on a greased baking tray cut side downwards. Brush the surface of each pepper with olive oil.
2 Roast the peppers in a preheated 200°C/400°F/gas mark 6 oven for 15–20 minutes or until the surfaces are blistering and the peppers are starting to soften.
3 Place the peppers in a large bowl and cover the bowl with clingfilm (plastic wrap). This makes the peppers easier to peel once they are cool.
4 Slice the lemon and remove any pips. Cut each lemon slice into four quarters and steam the lemon pieces for 5 minutes or until the skins are soft. Allow to cool.
5 Remove the skins from the peppers when cool, and cut the pepper flesh into strips.
6 Combine the pepper strips, lemon pieces, mint and olive oil. Season with black pepper and leave the salad to stand for a few hours before serving, to allow the flavours to combine.

Roasted Sweet Pepper, Artichoke and Olive Salad

Serves 4

This simple combination of salad ingredients works particularly well.

1 sweet red pepper
1 sweet yellow pepper
1tbsp olive oil
400g/14oz can artichoke hearts
10 black olives
2–3tbsp French Dressing, page 88
or good quality olive oil

1 Halve and deseed the sweet peppers and place cut side down on a greased baking tray.
2 Brush the surface of each pepper with olive oil.
3 Bake the peppers in a preheated 200°C/400°F/gas mark 6 oven for 15–20 minutes or until the skins are blistering and the peppers are starting to soften.
4 Place the peppers in a bowl and cover the bowl with clingfilm (plastic wrap). This makes the peppers easier to skin once they are cool.
5 Remove the skins from the peppers and cut the flesh into even-sized chunks. Place these in a bowl.
6 Drain the artichoke hearts and cut into quarters. Halve the black olives. Add to the roasted peppers. Mix well with the French dressing or olive oil and serve.

Mushroom and Tomato Salad

Serves 4

Mushrooms cooked in a herb-flavoured tomato sauce are served cold as a salad. They provide a lovely contrast when served as part of a selection of salads. This dish could also be served warm as a first course.

450g/1lb/4 cups button mushrooms
2 shallots
2 garlic cloves
1tbsp olive oil
4tbsp tomato paste
170ml/6fl oz/scant ¾ cup water
2tbsp finely chopped fresh mixed herbs e.g. basil, tarragon, parsley
salt and freshly ground black pepper

1 Halve or quarter the mushrooms if they are large.
2 Finely dice the shallots and crush the garlic clove.
3 Place the shallots and garlic in a saucepan with the olive oil and sweat them in the oil until the shallots begin to soften. Add the mushrooms and continue to sweat the vegetables until the mushrooms begin to soften.
4 Add the tomato paste and water, mix well and simmer for 5 minutes.
5 Add the fresh herbs and season to taste with salt and black pepper.
6 Allow the mixture to cool, then serve.

Chinese Orange Salad

Serves 4

This is another quick and easy salad whose ingredients complement each other well. I have not included a dressing with this salad but it goes well with the Tahini and Orange Dressing or the Tomato French Dressing (see index).

¼ head Chinese leaves	2 oranges
1 small bunch watercress	4 spring (green) onions
125g/4oz/1⅓ cups beansprouts	1tsp grated orange rind

1 Slice the Chinese leaves and mix with the watercress and beansprouts in a bowl.
2 Grate 1 teaspoon of rind from one of the oranges, then remove the peel from both. Cut the orange flesh into small pieces.
3 Cut the spring (green) onions into thin slices.
4 Add the orange flesh, grated orange rind and the sliced spring (green) onions to the salad. Mix and serve.

Fennel, Mango and Walnut Salad

Serves 4

The unusual combination of ingredients in this recipe produces a mouth-watering salad.

2 medium fennel
1 large mango
60g/2oz/⅔ cup walnuts

DRESSING
4tbsp orange juice
2tsp lemon juice
2tbsp olive oil
2tsp fennel seeds
2tsp grated fresh ginger
2tsp chopped fresh parsley

1 Remove the shoots from the fennel and cut the flesh into 5mm/¼ inch slices. Steam the fennel for 5–8 minutes or until almost cooked. Allow the fennel to cool.
2 Skin the mango, remove the stone and cut the flesh into small chunks.
3 Place the dressing ingredients in a large bowl and mix well to combine. Add the fennel, mango and walnuts and toss to coat before serving.

Red Bean, Avocado and Tomato Salad

Serves 4

This is a very simple, easy to make salad which produces a dish full of colour.

400g/14oz can red kidney beans
1 large avocado
12 cherry tomatoes
1 small red onion
1tbsp chopped fresh coriander (cilantro)
2tbsp French Dressing, page 88

1 Rinse and drain the kidney beans and place in a bowl.
2 Cut the avocado into chunks, halve the cherry tomatoes and slice the red onion. Add to the kidney beans.
3 Mix in the coriander (cilantro) and French dressing and serve.

Greek Tomato, Onion and Olive Salad

Serves 4

Tomatoes are much more enjoyable and full of flavour if they are well ripened, served at room temperature and preferably organically grown.

4 large ripe tomatoes
1 small red onion
12 olives
2–3tbsp good quality olive oil
freshly ground black pepper
1tbsp chopped fresh mint

1 Slice the tomatoes, finely slice the red onion and halve the olives.
2 Place a layer of tomato slices in a serving dish and sprinkle with olive oil and black pepper. Layer the onion slices on top, followed by the olives, sprinkling each layer with olive oil and black pepper. Sprinkle the fresh mint over the top.
3 Allow the salad to stand for 30 minutes before serving.

Beetroot, Orange and Olive Salad

Serves 4

This salad is based on a recipe which was given to me by an Italian patient. It is eaten in Italy with the addition of anchovies and lots of crusty bread to mop up the juices.

2 medium beetroot (beets)
½tsp grated orange rind
2 medium oranges
20 black olives
3tbsp good quality olive oil
1tbsp chopped fresh parsley
freshly ground black pepper

1. Cook, cool and skin the beetroot (beets). Cut into 1cm/½ inch dice.
2. Grate ½ teaspoon of peel from one of the oranges or grate the peel from both oranges and freeze all but ½ teaspoon for future use. Cut the remaining peel from the oranges using a sharp knife and cut the flesh into segments or chunks.
3. Combine the beetroot (beet) and orange flesh with the orange rind, black olives, olive oil and parsley. Season to taste with black pepper.
4. Leave the salad to stand before serving, preferably for a few hours, to allow the flavours to combine.

Grated Carrot and Red Chilli Salad

Serves 4

Provided that they are acceptable, roasted peanuts also work particularly well in this dish instead of the almonds or hazelnuts. This salad is the perfect accompaniment to vegetable curry and rice, but is also enjoyable served with a selection of different salads.

350g/12oz carrots
125g/4 oz/¾ cup almonds or hazelnuts
½ red chilli
1tbsp chopped fresh coriander (cilantro)
½ quantity Garlic Mayonnaise, page 90

1. Grate the carrots.
2. Toast the nuts in a medium oven or grill (broiler) and then roughly chop.
3. Deseed and finely dice the red chilli.
4. Combine the carrots, nuts, chilli, fresh coriander (cilantro) and the garlic mayonnaise. Leave the salad to stand for 30 minutes before serving, to allow the flavours to blend.

Oriental Rice Salad

Serves 4

This is a delightful way of serving brown rice. The addition of 1 tablespoon of shoyu sauce makes it even tastier. Use lemon juice if you cannot find fresh limes.

125g/4oz/heaping ½ cup brown rice
2tbsp sesame oil
2tbsp lime juice
1tsp grated fresh ginger
30g/1oz/¼ cup flaked almonds
30g/1oz/¼ cup sunflower seeds
60g/2oz/½ cup sesame seeds
freshly ground black pepper

1. Cook the brown rice in lots of water until tender. Drain well to remove excess water.
2. Add the sesame oil, lime juice and grated ginger to the rice while it is still warm. Allow the rice to cool.
3. Toast the almonds, sunflower seeds and sesame seeds, separately, in a medium oven or grill (broiler) until golden brown.
4. Add the nuts and seeds to the rice just before serving along with lots of black pepper.

MainCoursesMainCoursesMainC

rsesMainCourses

MainCourses

Chick Pea and Cashew Nut Korma

Serves 4

Some of the chick peas (garbanzo beans), onions and cashew nuts in this recipe are processed to produce a thick, creamy sauce, which binds the remaining ingredients together. Try substituting aubergine (eggplant) for the onions if these are not well tolerated.

2 large onions
1 garlic clove
2tsp olive oil
1tsp garam masala
1tsp ground cumin
1tsp ground coriander
½tsp ground cardamom
1tsp fennel seeds
1tsp turmeric
2tsp grated fresh ginger
60g/2oz creamed coconut
600ml/20fl oz/2½ cups boiling water
125g/4oz/scant 1 cup whole cashew nuts
420g/15oz can chick peas (garbanzo beans)
2 medium carrots
½ large sweet red pepper
½–1 x 227g/8oz can pineapple chunks
or 2 quartered tomatoes
1tbsp chopped fresh coriander (cilantro)
salt and freshly ground black pepper

1. Dice the onions and crush the garlic clove. Place in a saucepan with the olive oil and sweat them in the oil until the onion begins to soften. Add the spices and ginger and continue to sweat the ingredients for a few more minutes.
2. Dissolve the creamed coconut in the boiling water and add half of this to the onions and spices in the pan. Continue to cook until the onions are soft.
3. Place half of the onion mixture in a food processor along with half of the cashew nuts and half the chick peas (garbanzo beans). Process until smooth. If you do not have a food processor, mash the onions and chick peas (garbanzo beans) and add 60g/2oz/⅔ cup ground almonds instead of the cashews.

4 Add the remaining coconut milk, the cashew nuts and the chick peas (garbanzo beans) to the onions left in the pan. Cut the carrots into thin strips and the sweet pepper into small chunks. Add these to the pan, bring the mixture to the boil and simmer until the carrots and sweet pepper are tender.
5 Add the processed cashews, chick peas (garbanzo beans) and onions to the pan along with the drained pineapple chunks or quartered tomatoes and the fresh coriander (cilantro). Warm through, season to taste with salt and black pepper and serve with rice and salads. This dish can be frozen.

Winter Vegetable and Pumpkin Curry

Serves 4

The Pumpkin in this recipe produces a creamy sauce in which the vegetables are cooked. Beans could be substituted for some of the vegetables.

450g/1lb pumpkin flesh
2 onions
1 garlic clove
2tbsp olive oil
900g/2lb selection vegetables e.g. leeks, onions, parsnips, carrots, celeriac, swede, mushrooms, fennel
1tsp ground cumin
1tsp ground coriander
½tsp garam masala
½tsp ground cinnamon
½tsp ground fennel
¼tsp ground cardamom
½tsp paprika
½tsp ground ginger
60g/2oz creamed coconut
300ml/10fl oz/1¼ cups vegetable stock
salt and freshly ground black pepper

1. Cube the pumpkin flesh (you do not need to peel the pumpkin unless the skin is old and tough). Dice the onion and crush the garlic clove.
2. Place the pumpkin, onion and garlic in a saucepan with 1 tablespoon of olive oil and sweat the vegetables in the oil until they begin to soften. Cover the pan and continue to sweat the vegetables until the pumpkin is soft. Process or mash the pumpkin and onion mixture to a smooth purée.
3. Cut the vegetables into pieces that will cook in an equal amount of time. Place in a saucepan with the remaining 1 tablespoon of olive oil and sweat the vegetables until they begin to soften and brown.
4. Add the spices and cook for 2 minutes.
5. Dissolve the creamed coconut in the vegetable stock and add to the vegetables in the pan. Bring to the boil and simmer until the vegetables are just cooked.
6. Add the puréed pumpkin, mix well and continue to cook for another 5 minutes to allow the flavours to blend. Season with salt and black pepper and serve with rice and salads. This dish freezes well.

Lentil and Vegetable Curry

Serves 4

The lentils in this dish are puréed to produce a curry sauce in which the vegetables are cooked.

200g/7oz/1 cup split red lentils
1 litre/35fl oz/4½ cups water
780g/1¾lb selection of vegetables e.g. leeks, onions, fennel, celery, carrots, courgettes (zucchini), sweet peppers, mushrooms, sweetcorn, okra
2 garlic cloves
2.5cm/1in piece fresh ginger
1tbsp olive oil
1tsp ground cumin
1tsp ground coriander
½tsp garam masala
½tsp turmeric
¼tsp cayenne pepper
½tsp fennel seeds
¼tsp ground cardamom
salt and freshly ground black pepper

1. Cook the lentils for 1 hour in the water until soft and puréed.
2. Cut the vegetables into even-sized pieces. Crush the garlic cloves and grate the ginger.
3. Place the vegetables in a saucepan with the olive oil, garlic and ginger. Start with the vegetables which take the longest time to cook and sweat the vegetables until they all begin to soften.
4. Add the spices and cook for another 2 minutes.
5. Add the lentil purée, bring to the boil and simmer for approximately 15 minutes or until all the vegetables are well cooked. Add a little more water if the mixture becomes too dry. Season to taste with salt and black pepper. Serve with rice and salads. This curry is suitable for freezing.

Vegetable Rogan Josh

Serves 4

This rogan josh sauce is used as a 'cook in sauce' and is ideal for pouring over vegetables and beans or meat and fish for non-vegetarian family members. It is so easy to prepare that I make up double the quantity and freeze the excess. It makes a wonderful standby for quick and easy meals.

ROGAN JOSH SAUCE
3 medium onions
2.5cm/1in piece fresh ginger
1 large garlic clove
1tbsp olive oil
1tsp ground coriander
½tsp ground cardamom
¼tsp ground cloves
½tsp ground cinnamon
1tsp turmeric
⅓–½tsp chilli powder
60g/2oz creamed coconut
300ml/10fl oz/1¼ cups boiling water
300ml/10fl oz/1¼ cups passata (sieved tomatoes)
1tbsp chopped fresh coriander (cilantro)
salt and freshly ground black pepper

1 Finely dice the onion, grate the ginger and crush the garlic clove. Place in a saucepan with the olive oil and sweat them in the oil until the onion begins to soften and brown.
2 Add the ground coriander, cardamom, cloves, cinnamon, turmeric and chilli powder and sweat the ingredients for a few more minutes.
3 Dissolve the creamed coconut in the boiling water, place in a food processor along with two-thirds of the onion mixture and process until smooth. If you do not have a food processor, press two-thirds of the onion mixture through a sieve.
4 Place the processed mixture back into the pan and add the passata (sieved tomatoes) and fresh coriander (cilantro). Simmer for 5 minutes. Season with salt and black pepper and either freeze in containers ready for future use or use in one of the following recipes.

VARIATIONS

Cauliflower and Butter Bean Rogan Josh

Add 240ml/8fl oz/1 cup water, 350g/12oz cauliflower florets and 225g/8oz/heaping 1 cup cooked butter or lima beans to the above sauce and simmer for 30 minutes.

Mushroom and Leek Rogan Josh

Add 125ml/4fl oz/½ cup water, 350g/12oz leeks (mainly white stems, cut into 2.5cm/1 inch lengths) and 225g/8oz/2 cups button mushrooms to the sauce and simmer for 25 minutes.

Courgette and Chick Pea Rogan Josh

Add 350g/12oz sliced courgettes (zucchini) and 225g/8oz/heaping 1 cup cooked chick peas (garbanzo beans) to the sauce and simmer for 20 minutes.

Okra and Sweetcorn Rogan Josh

Add 125ml/4fl oz/½ cup water, 225g/8oz okra and 350g/12oz baby sweetcorn to the sauce and simmer for 20 minutes.

Fennel and Broccoli Rogan Josh

Add 240ml/8fl oz/1 cup water, 350g/12oz sliced fennel and 225g/8oz broccoli florets to the sauce and simmer for 30 minutes.

Egg Rogan Josh

Place halved, hard-boiled eggs on a bed of rice and pour the sauce over.

Leek and Lentil Bake

Serves 4

In this recipe, the lentils are puréed to make a creamy topping which is spread over the vegetables before baking.

- 2 medium onions
- 1 garlic clove
- 2tsp olive oil
- 225g/8oz/heaping 1 cup split red lentils
- 600ml/20fl oz/2½ cups water *or* vegetable stock
- 1 bayleaf
- ½tsp dried thyme
- 1tsp grated fresh ginger
- 1tsp garam masala
- ½tsp paprika
- ½tsp turmeric
- salt and freshly ground black pepper
- 680g/1½lbs leeks, white stems only
- 2tbsp chopped nuts to sprinkle

1 Finely dice the onions and crush the garlic clove. Place in a saucepan with the olive oil and sweat them in the oil until the onion begins to soften.

2 Add the lentils, water or stock, bayleaf, thyme, grated ginger, garam masala, paprika and turmeric. Bring to the boil and simmer until the lentils are soft and the water has been absorbed.

3 Remove the bayleaf, process the mixture in a food processor or mash until smooth. Season to taste with salt and black pepper.

4 Cut the leek stems into 2.5cm/1 inch lengths and steam for approximately 5 minutes or until the leeks are almost cooked.

5 Place the leeks in a gratin dish, pour the lentil mixture over and smooth the surface. Sprinkle the surface with chopped nuts.

6 Bake in a preheated 200°C/400°F/gas mark 6 oven for 20 minutes or until the topping is brown. Serve with baked potato or Chips (page 123) and a salad or vegetables. This recipe is suitable for freezing.

Vegetable and Chick Pea Bake

Serves 4

In this recipe, chick peas (garbanzo beans) are puréed to make a creamy topping that is spread over the vegetables before baking.

1.1kg/2½lb selection of vegetables e.g. onions, leeks, carrots, celeriac, broccoli, sweet peppers, mushrooms, sweetcorn, courgettes (zucchini), celery, fennel
2tsp olive oil
1tsp sesame oil
1 garlic clove

TOPPING
350g/12oz/scant 2 cups cooked chick peas (garbanzo beans)
3tbsp light tahini
½tsp dried marjoram
½tsp dried rosemary
½tsp dried thyme
1tbsp lemon juice
2 garlic cloves
salt and freshly ground black pepper
300ml/10fl oz/1¼ cups good quality vegetable stock
1tsp mustard
salt and freshly ground black pepper
1tbsp sesame seeds

1. Cut the vegetables into largish chunks, place in a saucepan with the oils and crushed garlic and sweat the vegetables in the oil until they are all starting to soften and brown. Start with the ones which take the longest time to cook.
2. Place the chick peas (garbanzo beans) in a food processor with the tahini, herbs, lemon juice, garlic, salt and black pepper. Process along with sufficient cooking liquid or water to produce a soft purée.
3. Place the vegetables in a gratin dish, mix the vegetable stock with the mustard and pour over the vegetables.
4. Spread the chick pea (garbanzo bean) purée evenly over the top of the vegetables and sprinkle the sesame seeds on the surface.
5. Bake in a preheated 200°C/400°F/gas mark 6 oven for 30–40 minutes or until the topping is brown and the vegetables are just cooked. Serve with salads. This recipe is suitable for freezing.

Vegetable Hotpot

Serves 4

In this recipe, cubes of potato are baked and browned on top of vegetables in a savoury sauce. For extra protein add some chick peas (garbanzo beans), butter or lima beans instead of some of the vegetables.

1.1kg/2½lb potatoes
1.1kg/2½lb selection of vegetables e.g. onions, leeks, celery, fennel, carrots, parsnips, celeriac, courgettes (zucchini), broccoli, cabbage, sweet peppers, aubergine (eggplant), mushrooms, broad (fava) beans, French beans
2 garlic cloves
3tbsp olive oil
1tsp dried thyme
1tsp dried rosemary
2tsp paprika
1tbsp chopped fresh parsley
1 bayleaf
1tsp mustard powder
3tbsp rice flour
1tbsp tomato paste
140ml/5fl oz/⅔ cup cold water
425ml/15fl oz/2 cups vegetable stock
salt and freshly ground black pepper

1 Peel the potatoes and cut into 1cm/½ inch dice. Steam the diced potato for 10 minutes. Remove from the steam and leave to cool and dry.
2 Cut the vegetables into even-sized chunks. Crush the garlic cloves. Place the vegetables and garlic in a casserole dish or saucepan with 1 tablespoon of the olive oil and sweat the vegetables in the oil for approximately 5 minutes. Do not overcook.
3 Add the thyme, rosemary, paprika, parsley and the bayleaf to the vegetables. Mix the mustard powder, rice flour and tomato paste with the cold water until smooth. Add the vegetable stock and mix well. Pour this mixture on to the vegetables and bring to the boil, stirring constantly. Season with salt and black pepper. Transfer to an ovenproof dish if necessary.

4 Place the potato in a bowl with the remaining 2 tablespoons of olive oil and toss until well coated. Season with salt and black pepper.
5 Pile the potatoes on top of the vegetables.
6 Bake near the top of a preheated 200°C/400°F/gas mark 6 oven for 45 minutes. The potatoes should be brown on top. Place under the grill (broiler) for 5 minutes if they are not sufficiently browned. Serve with salads.

Potato, Leek and Celeriac Hotpot

Serves 4

In this recipe, cubes of potato are baked and browned on top of a creamy sauce of leeks and celeriac.

900g/2lb peeled potatoes
565g/1¼lb peeled celeriac
565g/1¼lb leeks, mainly white stems
3tbsp olive oil
300ml/10fl oz/1¼ cups soya milk
3tbsp rice flour
1tsp mustard powder
300ml/10fl oz/1¼ cups vegetable stock
1 bayleaf
½tsp grated fresh nutmeg
½tsp lemon rind
1tbsp finely chopped fresh parsley
1tbsp finely chopped fresh dill
1tbsp finely chopped fresh fennel
or ½tsp of each of the above herbs, dried
salt and freshly ground black pepper

1 Cut the peeled potatoes and celeriac into 1cm/½ inch cubes. Steam separately for 10 minutes each.
2 Slice the leeks into 2.5cm/1 inch lengths, place in a saucepan with the olive oil and sweat the leek in the oil until beginning to soften. Mix together the soya milk, rice flour and mustard powder and add to the pan along with the stock, bayleaf, nutmeg and lemon rind. Bring to the boil and simmer for 2 minutes.
3 Remove the bayleaf from the sauce and add the celeriac. Add the parsley, dill and fennel and mix well. Season to taste, then place the mixture in a large, greased gratin dish.
4 Toss the cubes of potato in the remaining 2 tablespoons of olive oil until well coated. Season with salt and black pepper and spread over the celeriac and leek mixture.
5 Bake in a preheated 190°C/375°F/gas mark 5 oven for 45–60 minutes or until the potatoes are well cooked and golden brown. If not browning sufficiently, finish off under the grill (broiler).

Creamy Butter Bean, Aubergine and Potato Casserole

Serves 4

I love to make casseroles in winter. This one is a meal in itself as potatoes are included in the recipe. I use canned butter or lima beans when I am in a hurry. The tofu is optional but adds an interesting texture and more protein to the casserole.

4 medium onions
565g/1¼lb potatoes
4 medium carrots
1 large aubergine (eggplant)
5cm/2in piece fresh ginger
2tbsp olive oil
4tbsp tahini
850ml/30fl oz/3¾ cups vegetable stock
½ x 285g/10oz packet plain tofu
450g/1lb/heaping 2 cups cooked butter *or* lima beans
2tbsp chopped fresh coriander (cilantro)
2tbsp chopped fresh mint
2tbsp chopped fresh parsley
½tsp grated nutmeg
salt and freshly ground black pepper

1. Quarter the onions, cut the potatoes and carrots into large chunks and the aubergine (eggplant) into large dice. Grate the ginger and place in a large casserole dish or saucepan with the vegetables and olive oil. Sweat the vegetables in the oil until they begin to soften. Transfer to an ovenproof dish if necessary.
2. Dissolve the tahini in the stock and add to the vegetables along with the cubed tofu, cooked butter or lima beans, fresh herbs and grated nutmeg.
3. Cook the casserole in a preheated 170°C/325°F/gas mark 3 oven for approximately 1½ hours or until the vegetables are soft and some of the ingredients have broken down to produce a thick sauce. Add a little more liquid during cooking if the sauce is becoming too dry. Season to taste with salt and black pepper and serve with salads.

Aduki Bean and Red Cabbage Casserole

Serves 4

For special occasions, and for those allowed, substitute 140ml/5fl oz/⅔ cup red wine for some of the stock or water. The fresh herbs can be mixed with butter or margarine to make a herb butter, which is delicious melted on top of the casserole.

175g/6oz/scant 1 cup aduki beans	850ml/30fl oz/3¾ cups vegetable stock *or* water
175g/6oz mushrooms	1tsp caraway seeds
1 garlic clove	2tsp dried dill
4tsp olive oil	2tbsp raisins
450g/1lb red cabbage	salt and freshly ground black pepper
3 medium red onions	2tbsp fresh mint, chives, chervil *or* parsley, *or* a mixture
2tbsp tahini	
2tbsp tomato paste	

1. Soak the aduki beans for at least 3 hours in lots of boiling water. Rinse well, cover with boiling water and cook for approximately 40 minutes or until soft. If using a pressure cooker this will take approximately 5 minutes.
2. Leave the mushrooms whole if small, halve or quarter them if large. Crush the garlic clove.
3. Place the mushrooms and garlic in a saucepan or casserole dish with 2 teaspoons of the olive oil and sweat them until the mushrooms begin to soften. Remove from the pan.
4. Cut the red cabbage into rough chunks and the onions into large segments. Add the onions and red cabbage to the pan with the remaining oil and sweat these until they are just starting to soften.
5. Stir the tahini and tomato paste into a little water or stock to dissolve. Add to the pan along with the remaining stock or water, the mushrooms, aduki beans, caraway seeds, dill and the raisins. Transfer to an ovenproof dish if necessary.

6 Place in a preheated 200°C/400°F/gas mark 6 oven for 1–1¼ hours or until the vegetables and beans are cooked and most of the liquid has been absorbed.
7 Season with salt and black pepper, stir in the fresh herbs and serve. This is delicious served with a green salad and Chips (see below).

Chips

Serves 4

4 large potatoes | 2tbsp olive oil

1 Peel the potatoes and cut into chips (chunky French fries). Dry on a tea towel.
2 Place the chips in a large bowl with the olive oil and toss until the chips are all coated.
3 Place in rows on 1 or 2 greased baking trays, leaving a little gap between each chip.
4 Bake in a preheated 200°C/400°F/gas mark 6 oven for 30–40 minutes until golden and crisp.

Vegetable and Ginger Casserole with Herb Dumplings

Serves 4

This is a wonderful casserole for cold winter days – filling, warming and comforting.

1.1kg/2½lbs selection of vegetables e.g. swede, parsnip, carrots, onions, leeks, broccoli, courgette (zucchini), celery, fennel, mushrooms, sweet peppers, pumpkin, celeriac
3.5cm/1½in piece fresh ginger
400g/14oz can chopped tomatoes
850ml/30fl oz/3¾ cups water
1tsp paprika
1tsp fennel seeds
½tsp dried thyme
1tsp celery seeds
1tbsp chopped fresh coriander (cilantro)
1tbsp chopped fresh parsley
salt and freshly ground black pepper

HERB DUMPLINGS
175g/6oz/1 cup well cooked rice
4tsp sunflower oil
125–180ml/4–6fl oz/½–¾ cup water
90g/3oz/9tbsp rice flour
2tsp baking powder
¼tsp dried thyme
salt and freshly ground black pepper

1 Cut the vegetables into large chunks that will cook in roughly the same amount of time.
2 Slice the ginger into very thin pieces.
3 Place the tomatoes, water, spices, herbs, salt and black pepper into a casserole dish and mix. Add the vegetables and ginger.
4 Cook in a preheated oven, 200°C/400°F/gas mark 6, for 1¼ hours.
5 Meanwhile, make the dumplings. Place the rice, oil and 125ml/4fl oz/½ cup of water in a food processor and process until smooth.

Add the rice flour, baking powder, thyme and salt and black pepper. Process again, adding sufficient of the remaining 125ml/2fl oz/½ cup of water to make a soft dough. The amount of water will depend on how well cooked the rice is.

6 Divide the mixture into 12 dumplings and roll each in a little rice flour.
7 Move the vegetables to the centre of the casserole dish and place the dumplings around the side in the juices. Return to the oven and cook for another 15–20 minutes. Serve with salads, baked potatoes or Chips (page 123).

Carrot and Celeriac Bake

Serves 4

This adaptable recipe can be altered to suit varying tastes. Parsnips can be substituted for the carrot or celeriac, oat flakes could be used instead of millet flakes if gluten does not cause problems and, if acceptable, grated cheese mixed with breadcrumbs can be sprinkled on the surface to produce a crispy bake.

450g/1lb carrots
450g/1lb celeriac
2 large *or* 3 medium eggs
½tsp dried thyme *or* 1tbsp fresh thyme
1tbsp fresh *or* frozen coriander (cilantro)
¼tsp grated fresh nutmeg
salt and freshly ground black pepper
60g/2oz millet flakes

1. Cut the carrots and celeriac into equal-sized pieces. Boil or steam until just tender.
2. Place the vegetables in a food processor and process until smooth. Mash the vegetables if you do not have a food processor. Allow to cool.
3. Beat the eggs and add the thyme, coriander (cilantro), nutmeg, salt and black pepper. Mix the eggs into the vegetables along with the millet flakes.
4. Place the mixture in a well-greased gratin dish. Bake in a preheated 180°C/350°F/gas mark 4 oven for 35–40 minutes until set. Serve with baked potatoes and salads.

Carrot, Parsnip and Cashew Nut Roast

Serves 4

This roast is delicious served with Tomato Sauce or Red Onion Gravy (see index). Quinoa or rice could be substituted for the millet grain if desired.

450g/1lb carrots
90g/3oz/scant ½ cup millet grain
125g/4oz/⅔ cup cashew nuts
1 onion
1 garlic clove
1tbsp olive oil
175g/6oz parsnips
1tsp dried sage
1tsp dried thyme
1tbsp chopped fresh parsley
salt and freshly ground black pepper

1. Cook the carrots until soft, place in a food processor and process. Mash them if you do not have a food processor.
2. Cook the millet in lots of water until soft, approximately 20 minutes. Sieve to remove excess water.
3. Toast the cashew nuts lightly in a medium oven or grill (broiler).
4. Dice the onion and crush the garlic clove. Place in a saucepan with the olive oil and sweat them in the oil for 3–4 minutes.
5. Grate the parsnips and add to the onion in the pan. Continue to cook over a medium heat, stirring occasionally, until the parsnips and onion are nicely browned. This will take approximately 20 minutes, do not rush and do not turn the heat up too high.
6. Add the onion and parsnip mixture, the cashew nuts, millet, and herbs to the puréed carrots. Mix well and season with salt and black pepper.
7. Place in a greased and lined 900g/2lb loaf tin (pan). Cover the surface loosely with foil and bake in a preheated 180°C/350°F/gas mark 4 oven for approximately 40 minutes. Serve with a sauce and salads, vegetables, potatoes or rice. This roast freezes well.

Creamy Cashew Nut and Almond Roast

Serves 4

In this recipe the cashew nuts, carrot and onion are processed to produce a thick sauce, which holds the remaining vegetables and nuts together. The result is a soft, creamy nut roast that can also be served cold as a pâté. I have given the weights for the vegetables, as it is quite important that the quantities are correct.

225g/8oz onion
1 garlic clove
4tsp olive oil
125g/4oz carrot
125g/4oz/⅔ cup cashew nuts
4tsp tomato paste
125g/4oz sweet red pepper
60g/2oz celery
175g/6oz courgettes (zucchini)
125g/4oz/⅔ cup almonds
¾tsp dried rosemary
¾tsp dried thyme
salt and freshly ground black pepper

1 Finely dice the onion and crush the garlic clove. Place in a saucepan with 2 teaspoons of the olive oil and sweat them in the oil until the onion begins to soften.
2 Grate the carrot and add to the pan. Cover with a lid and continue to sweat the vegetables until the carrot and onion are soft.
3 Place the carrot and onion in a food processor with the cashew nuts and tomato paste and process until quite smooth. If you do not have a food processor, mash the vegetables and use ground almonds instead of the cashews.
4 Roughly chop the almonds.
5 Finely dice the sweet pepper and celery and grate the courgettes (zucchini). Place the sweet pepper and celery in a saucepan with 2 teaspoons of olive oil and sweat them in the oil for for a few minutes. Add the courgettes (zucchini) and continue to sweat the vegetables until they begin to soften.
6 Add the herbs to the pan along with the processed carrot and onion mixture and the almonds. Mix well and season with salt and black pepper.

7 Place in a greased and lined 900g/2lb loaf tin (pan) and bake in a preheated 180°C/350°F/gas mark 4 oven for ¾–1 hour or until golden brown. The centre should still feel soft to the touch.
8 Allow the loaf to cool for 10–15 minutes in the pan before turning out and removing the lining paper. Serve with baked potatoes or Chips (page 123) and salads or vegetables. This recipe is suitable for freezing.

Pasta with Mushrooms and Tomato Sauce

Serves 4

This is a really quick and easy meal to prepare yet it looks delightful and is quite delicious. Grated cheese can be sprinkled on top for added flavour, if acceptable.

TOMATO SAUCE
½ onion
600ml/20fl oz/2½ cups passata (sieved tomatoes)
1tsp dried basil
½tsp dried oregano
1 bayleaf

285g/10oz wheat-free pasta
450g/1lb mushrooms
1 garlic clove
1tbsp olive oil
¼tsp each dried basil, oregano, thyme, paprika and rosemary

1 To make the tomato sauce, finely dice the onion and place in a pan with the remaining sauce ingredients, bring to the boil and simmer for 10 minutes. Remove the bayleaf and keep warm.
2 Cook the pasta according to the instructions on the packet and keep warm.
3 Wash the mushrooms and cut in half or quarter depending on their size. Crush the garlic clove.
4 Gently heat the oil in a frying pan, add the garlic, herbs and spices and fry for 1 minute.
5 Add the mushrooms and stir-fry over a gentle heat for 2–3 minutes until they are just beginning to soften. Season with salt and black pepper.
6 Serve the tomato sauce on a bed of pasta with the mushrooms piled on top.

Fresh Herb Risotto with Sun-Dried Tomatoes and Olives

Serves 4

I keep ready-cooked rice in the freezer so that I can make this risotto quickly and easily. Just place the rice in a sieve and pour boiling water over it. Use frozen herbs if you do not have any fresh.

5cm/2in piece fresh ginger
4 garlic cloves
bunch of spring (green) onions *or* 1 large onion
4tsp olive oil
2tsp sesame oil
900g/2lbs/5⅓ cups cooked rice
125ml/4fl oz/½ cup water
2tbsp chopped fresh basil
2tbsp chopped fresh coriander (cilantro)
2tbsp chopped fresh parsley
8 large sun-dried tomatoes
20 black olives
salt and freshly ground black pepper

1. Cut the ginger into very thin slices, crush the garlic cloves and slice the spring (green) onions or dice the ordinary onion.
2. Place the ginger, garlic and onion in a saucepan with the olive and sesame oils and sweat them in the oil until they are soft.
3. Add the cooked rice, water and chopped herbs. Cut the sun-dried tomatoes into small pieces and halve the olives, and add these along with the salt and black pepper.
4. Simmer for approximately 5 minutes or until the water has been absorbed and the risotto has warmed through. Serve with salad.

Lentil and Walnut Burgers with Tomato Sauce

Serves 4

Lentils cooked until they form a thick purée are used in this recipe to hold the vegetables and herbs together in a burger shape.

2 medium onions
2 garlic cloves
175g/6oz/scant 1 cup red split lentils
425ml/15fl oz/2 cups water
½tsp dried rosemary
½tsp dried thyme
1 bayleaf
3tbsp tomato paste
125g/4oz/1⅓ cups walnuts, finely chopped
salt and freshly ground black pepper
1tbsp each of sesame seeds and rice flour for coating
olive oil for brushing

TOMATO SAUCE
1 small onion
1 garlic clove
2tsp olive oil
400g/14oz can chopped tomatoes
½tsp dried basil
½tsp dried oregano
140ml/5fl oz/⅔ cup water

1 Finely dice the onions and crush the garlic cloves.
2 Place the onions and garlic, lentils, water and herbs into a saucepan and bring to the boil. Simmer, covered, stirring occasionally until the lentils are soft and the mixture starts to become a thick purée. This should take approximately 40 minutes.
3 Remove the bayleaf. Stir in the tomato paste and walnuts, then add salt and black pepper to taste. Allow the mixture to cool.
4 Sprinkle the sesame seeds and rice flour on to a work surface. Divide the lentil mixture into eight, roll each portion into the flour and seeds, and then flatten into a burger shape.

5 Place the burgers on a greased baking tray. Brush the surface with olive oil and bake in a preheated 200°C/400°F/gas mark 6 oven for approximately 25 minutes or until the burgers are beginning to brown.
6 Meanwhile, prepare the tomato sauce. Finely dice the onion and crush the garlic clove. Place in a saucepan with the olive oil and sweat them in the oil until the onion begins to soften and brown.
7 Add the tomatoes, herbs and water, bring to the boil and simmer for 30 minutes. Serve immediately with the lentil and walnut burgers. The burgers and sauce can be frozen (in separate containers).

Carrot and Hazelnut Rissoles with Red Onion Gravy

Serves 4

My original recipe for these rissoles contained wheat and is an interesting variation if wheat is acceptable. Replace the millet cooked in carrot juice with 90g/3oz/½ cup couscous soaked in 200ml/7fl oz/¾ cup of carrot juice and add 90g/3oz/1½ cups wholewheat breadcrumbs instead of the millet flakes.

90g/3oz/scant ½ cup millet grain
500ml/18fl oz/2¼ cups carrot juice
225g/8oz peeled carrots
1 small onion
1 garlic clove
2tsp olive oil
½tsp paprika
½tsp turmeric
1tsp ground coriander
½tsp ground cumin
1 egg, beaten
30g/1oz millet flakes
90g/3oz/⅔ cup hazelnuts
salt and freshly ground black pepper
rice flour for coating

RED ONION GRAVY
2 medium onions
1tbsp olive oil
300ml/10fl oz/1¼ cups vegetable stock
1tbsp tomato paste
1tsp mustard
1 bayleaf
salt and freshly ground black pepper

1. Place the millet in a saucepan with the carrot juice and simmer, covered, for approximately 30 minutes or until the millet is well cooked and the carrot juice has been absorbed. The mixture should still be quite moist. Allow the mixture to cool.
2. Finely grate the carrots, finely dice the onion and crush the garlic clove. Place in a saucepan with the olive oil and sweat them in the oil until they begin to soften.

3 Add the carrot and onion mixture to the cooked millet along with the paprika, turmeric, ground coriander, cumin, beaten egg, millet flakes and the finely ground hazelnuts. Mix well and season with salt and black pepper.
4 Divide the mixture into eight and form into balls by rolling in rice floured hands. Press into burger shapes and place on a greased baking tray.
5 Brush the surface of each rissole with olive oil and bake in a pre-heated 200°C/400°F/gas mark 6 oven for approximately 25 minutes or until browning around the edges.
6 Meanwhile, prepare the gravy. Halve the onions, cut into very thin slices and place in a saucepan with the olive oil. Slowly sweat the onion slices in the oil, over a medium heat, until they are soft and brown. This process will take approximately 30 minutes, do not rush, and stir regularly.
7 Add the vegetable stock, tomato paste, mustard and bayleaf. Bring to the boil and simmer until it forms a thick sauce. Remove the bayleaf and season to taste with salt and black pepper. Serve the rissoles hot with the red onion gravy. The rissoles and onion gravy can both be frozen.

Parsnip, Leek and Carrot Terrine with Tomato Sauce

Serves 4

Other vegetables can be used in this recipe, for example celeriac instead of the parsnips or carrots, and broccoli or spinach instead of the leeks.

450g/1lb parsnips
450g/1lb carrots
450g/1lb leeks
1tsp grated ginger
1tsp grated orange rind
1tbsp fresh coriander (cilantro)
3 eggs
salt and freshly ground black pepper
1 quantity Tomato Sauce, page 132

1 Cut the vegetables into pieces and cook each vegetable separately by boiling or steaming until tender.
2 Purée or process the vegetables separately in a food processor, adding the ginger to the parsnips, the orange rind to the carrots and the coriander (cilantro) to the leeks. Add 1 egg to each mixture and season with salt and black pepper.
3 Grease and line a 900g/2lb loaf tin (pan). Spread the carrot mixture evenly on the base of the tin (pan), then the leek mixture and finally the parsnip mixture on the top.
4 Place the loaf pan in a baking tray of cold water (a bain-marie or water bath) and bake in a preheated 200°C/400°F/gas mark 6 oven for 40–50 minutes or until a knife inserted in the centre comes out clean.
5 Stand for 10 minutes before turning out. Cut into slices to serve, accompanied by the tomato sauce.

Pasta with Julienne Vegetables and Pine Nuts

Serves 4

Wheat-free pasta is now readily available made from other grains.

1 garlic clove
2.5cm/1in piece fresh ginger, optional
2 carrots
2 courgettes (zucchini)
1 sweet red pepper
225g/8oz broccoli
125g/4oz asparagus, mangetout (snowpeas) or green beans
8 spring (green) onions
125g/4oz whole baby sweetcorn
350g/12oz wheat-free pasta
1tbsp olive oil
1tsp unbleached corn flour (cornstarch)
350ml/12fl oz/1½ cups vegetable stock
1tbsp chopped fresh parsley
1tbsp chopped fresh tarragon
1tbsp chopped fresh basil
1tsp grated lemon rind
4 sun-dried tomatoes, optional
salt and freshly ground black pepper
30g/1oz/heaping ¼ cup toasted pine nuts

1. Crush the garlic clove and finely slice the ginger. Cut the carrots, courgettes (zucchini) and sweet pepper into thin strips approximately 1 x 5cm/¼ x 2 inches. Cut the broccoli into florets, the asparagus and spring (green) onions into 2.5cm/1 inch lengths and the sweetcorn in half lengthways.
2. Cook the pasta according to the directions and keep warm.
3. Place the carrots, broccoli, ginger and garlic in a saucepan with the olive oil and sweat the vegetables for 3–4 minutes. Add the remaining vegetables and sweat them until they begin to soften.
4. Mix the corn flour (cornstarch) with a little vegetable stock and add to the vegetables along with the remaining stock, fresh herbs and lemon rind. Finely dice the sun-dried tomatoes, if using, and add to the pan. Bring to the boil and simmer for 1–2 minutes.
5. Add the pasta to the vegetables, stir to mix, season with salt and black pepper and sprinkle with pine nuts before serving.

Vegetable Lasagne

Serves 4–6

Lasagne does take time to prepare so do not attempt it if you are in a hurry. This recipe makes four generous portions, which I like to serve with salad and baked potatoes. It would easily stretch to serve six for supper. Lasagne is now available in wheat-free form but for those able to eat wheat and dairy produce normal pasta could be used and the surface sprinkled with grated cheese and breadcrumbs to give a golden crunchy topping.

TOMATO SAUCE
1 large onion
2 garlic cloves
2tsp olive oil
2 x 400g/14oz cans chopped tomatoes
1tsp dried basil
1tsp dried oregano
300ml/10fl oz/1¼ cups water

WHITE SAUCE
5tbsp rice flour
1 rounded tbsp mustard
¼tsp grated nutmeg
333ml/12fl oz/1½ cups soya milk
1 bayleaf
30g/1oz/2tbsp margarine
salt and freshly ground black pepper

780g/1¾lb selection vegetables e.g. broccoli, celery *or* fennel, aubergine (eggplant), sweet green *or* red peppers, mushrooms, courgettes (zucchini), carrots, sweetcorn, onions, celeriac

2tsp olive oil
90g/3oz olives, sun-dried tomatoes *or* dried apricots *or* a mixture of all three
6 sheets lasagne
3tbsp chopped nuts, to garnish

1 First make the tomato sauce. Finely dice the onion and crush the garlic cloves. Place in a saucepan with the olive oil and sweat them in the oil until the onion begins to soften and brown.

2 Add the tomatoes, herbs and water, bring to the boil and simmer for 30–40 minutes until the sauce is thick.
3 Cut the vegetables into chunks that will cook in a similar amount of time.
4 Add the vegetables to a pan with the olive oil and sweat them until they begin to soften. Cut the olives, sun-dried tomatoes or apricots into small pieces and add to the pan. Add the tomato sauce and mix well.
5 Now make the white sauce. Place the rice flour, mustard and nutmeg in a saucepan and mix with a little of the soya milk until smooth. Add the remaining soya milk, the bayleaf and margarine and bring to the boil, stirring constantly. Simmer for 2 minutes, then remove the bayleaf. Season to taste with salt and black pepper, cover the pan and remove from the heat until needed.
6 Assemble the lasagne. Place one quarter of the vegetable mixture in a lasagne dish and cover with a layer of lasagne. Place another quarter of the vegetable mixture on top. Pour over about half of the white sauce. Repeat these layers, using the remaining white sauce for the top layer.
7 Sprinkle the surface with chopped nuts and bake in a preheated 200°C/400°F/gas mark 6 oven for approximately 45 minutes (the cooking time will depend on the type of lasagne used).

Roasted Vegetables with Pasta and Almond Pesto Dressing

Serves 4

This recipe is made even more delicious with 1 tablespoon of balsamic vinegar added to the olive oil when coating the vegetables and another added to the pesto dressing. Try this if balsamic vinegar is an acceptable ingredient. If you do not like pesto sauce, Tomato Sauce (page 132) would make a good alternative.

4tbsp olive oil
2 large garlic cloves
salt and freshly ground black pepper
8 small onions
2 large courgettes (zucchini)
2 medium carrots
1 large sweet red pepper
1 large fennel
1 medium aubergine (eggplant)
350g/12oz wheat-free pasta

ALMOND PESTO DRESSING
60g/2oz fresh basil
1 small shallot
½tsp mustard
1 garlic clove
60g/2oz/scant ½ cup blanched toasted almonds
1tbsp lemon juice
150ml/5fl oz/⅔ cup good quality olive oil
salt and freshly ground black pepper

1 Place the olive oil in a large bowl. Crush the garlic cloves and add to the bowl along with a little salt and black pepper.
2 Cut the onions into halves, the courgettes (zucchini) and carrots into chunks, the sweet pepper into 8 pieces, the fennel into 8 segments and the aubergine (eggplant) into 1cm/½ inch slices.
3 Place the vegetables in the bowl containing the olive oil and garlic and toss until well coated. Place the vegetables on 2 greased baking trays and bake in a preheated 200°C/400°F/gas mark 6 oven for 30–40 minutes or until the vegetables are cooked and beginning to brown.
4 Cook the pasta according to the instructions and keep warm.

5 Prepare the pesto dressing. Place all the ingredients in a food processor and process until the sauce is smooth. If you do not have a food processor, finely chop the basil, shallots and garlic and use ground almonds instead of the toasted almonds. Mix to combine.
6 Serve the roasted vegetables piled on top of the pasta with the pesto sauce to accompany. Serve with salad.

Roasted Vegetables with Polenta or Rice

Follow the above recipe using polenta or rice instead of the pasta.

Almond and Ginger Stir-Fry

Serves 4

Strictly speaking, this recipe is not a stir-fry as I prefer to 'sweat' vegetables rather than stir-fry them (see page 45). Add 2 tablespoons of shoyu sauce and 1 tablespoon of chilli sauce to this dish for extra flavour, if acceptable.

125g/4oz/1⅓ cups flaked almonds
5cm/2in piece fresh ginger
2 garlic cloves
227g/8oz can water chestnuts
1 bunch spring (green) onions
1 large sweet red pepper
125g/4oz courgettes (zucchini) *or* broccoli florets
285g/10oz packet smoked tofu
125g/4oz baby sweetcorn
125g/4oz sugar snap peas, *or* mangetout (snowpeas)
125g/4oz mushrooms
1tbsp olive oil
1tsp sesame oil
1tbsp unbleached corn flour (cornstarch)
300ml/10fl oz/1¼ cups vegetable stock
1tbsp chopped fresh basil
1tbsp chopped fresh coriander (cilantro)
salt and freshly ground black pepper

1. Toast the almonds in a medium oven or grill (broiler) until golden.
2. Slice the ginger and crush the garlic cloves. Drain the water chestnuts.
3. Slice the spring (green) onions into 2.5cm/1 inch lengths and the sweet pepper, courgettes (zucchini) and smoked tofu into strips. Cut the baby sweetcorn in half lengthways. Top and tail the peas. Leave the mushrooms whole if small, otherwise cut in half.
4. In a large flat pan or wok gently heat the olive and sesame oil. Add the garlic and ginger, then the vegetables, one at a time, starting with the toughest ones first. Sweat the vegetables, stirring occasionally, until they begin to soften. Add the water chestnuts and tofu.
5. Mix the corn flour (cornstarch) with the vegetable stock and add to the pan along with the fresh herbs and toasted almonds. Bring to the boil, stirring, and then simmer until the vegetables are just cooked. Season with salt and black pepper and serve with rice and salads.

Sweet and Sour Green Lentils

Serves 4

This quick and easy dish has an interesting combination of textures and flavours. Add 2 tablespoons of shoyu or tamari sauce and 1 tablespoon of balsamic vinegar for extra flavour, if these ingredients are acceptable.

175g/6oz/scant 1 cup green lentils
1 large onion
2 garlic cloves
2.5cm/1in piece fresh ginger
1tbsp olive oil
1 large carrot
½ sweet red pepper
½ sweet green pepper
425ml/15fl oz/2 cups passata (sieved tomatoes)
227g/8oz can pineapple chunks in natural juice
285g/10oz packet tofu (plain *or* smoked)
salt and freshly ground black pepper

1 Cover the lentils with boiling water and cook for approximately 20 minutes or until soft. Drain.
2 Dice the onion, crush the garlic clove and finely slice the ginger. Place in a saucepan with the olive oil and sweat them in the oil until the onion begins to soften and brown.
3 Cut the carrot into matchstick pieces and the sweet peppers into slices. Add to the pan and continue to sweat the vegetables for another 5 minutes.
4 Add the lentils, passata (sieved tomatoes) and pineapple chunks and juice. Cube the tofu and add to the pan. Bring to the boil and simmer for 5–10 minutes until the vegetables are cooked and the mixture is well blended. Season with salt and black pepper and serve with rice and salad. This dish can be frozen.

Spiced Chick Peas with Spinach and Aubergine

Serves 4

This recipe is delicious with a little plain yogurt swirled through before serving.

1 large aubergine (eggplant)
2 large onions
2 garlic cloves
2tsp grated fresh ginger
4tsp olive oil
2tsp ground cumin
2tsp ground coriander
1tsp turmeric
1tsp paprika
½tsp cayenne pepper
½tsp ground cinnamon
90g/3oz creamed coconut
600ml/20fl oz/2½ cups boiling water
1tbsp tomato paste
2tsp lemon juice
1tsp lemon rind
225g/8oz/heaping 1 cup cooked chick peas (garbanzo beans)
225g/8oz spinach
1tbsp chopped fresh coriander (cilantro)
2 tomatoes, optional
salt and freshly ground black pepper
chopped fresh mint, to garnish

1 Dice the aubergine (eggplant) and onions and crush the garlic cloves.
2 Place the aubergine (eggplant), onions, garlic and ginger in a saucepan with the olive oil and sweat them in the oil until they begin to soften.
3 Add the spices and cook for another 2 minutes.
4 Dissolve the creamed coconut in the boiling water and add to the pan along with the tomato paste, lemon juice, lemon rind and chick peas (garbanzo beans). Bring to the boil, cover and simmer for 10 minutes.
5 Chop the spinach and add to the pan along with the fresh coriander (cilantro). Either transfer to a casserole dish and cook in a preheated 180°C/350°F/gas mark 4 oven for 45 minutes, or continue to

simmer, covered, on the top of the cooker for approximately 30 minutes or until the aubergine (eggplant) is soft. Add a little more water if the mixture starts to dry out before it is cooked.

6 Quarter the fresh tomatoes and add to the casserole. Season with salt and black pepper and mix well. Leave to stand for a few minutes to allow the tomatoes to warm through and just start to soften.
7 Garnish with the chopped mint and serve with rice, millet or quinoa and a green salad. This recipe is suitable for freezing.

Three Bean Chilli

Serves 4

This dish should really be called two bean chilli as lentils are not beans, but I'd become used to its name by the time I realised my mistake.

60g/2oz/heaping ¼ cup aduki beans
60g/2oz/heaping ¼ cup red kidney beans
60g/2oz/heaping ¼ cup whole red lentils
1 large onion
1 sweet green pepper
1 large carrot
1 green chilli
1 garlic clove
2tsp olive oil
600ml/20fl oz/2½ cups passata (sieved tomatoes)
1 bayleaf
1tsp dried basil
1tsp dried oregano
salt and freshly ground black pepper
¼–½tsp chilli powder

1. Soak the beans and lentils overnight in lots of water. Rinse, cover with water, bring to the boil and simmer until the beans are tender. Alternatively, pressure cook the pulses for 5 minutes.
2. Finely dice all the vegetables. Deseed and dice the chilli and crush the garlic clove. Place the vegetables, chilli and garlic in a saucepan with the olive oil and sweat them in the oil until they begin to soften. Add the passata (sieved tomatoes), herbs, spices, the beans and their cooking liquid, plus sufficient water, if necessary, to make a runny sauce.
3. Bring to the boil and simmer until all the vegetables and beans are tender and the sauce is thick. The lentils and beans should start to break up to form part of the sauce. Season with salt and black pepper and serve. This recipe is suitable for freezing.

Spaghetti Bolognaise

Serves 4

This is an unusual method of producing spaghetti bolognaise, where the sauce and spaghetti are cooked together, resulting in very succulent spaghetti. Organic soya mince is available in which no chemical solvents, flavourings or colourings are used.

- 2 large onions
- 2 medium carrots
- 2 garlic cloves
- 4tsp olive oil
- 4 large sun-dried tomatoes
- 175g/6oz soya mince (T.V.P.)
- 140g/5oz can tomato paste
- 1.75 litres/60fl oz/7½ cups vegetable stock or water
- 2tsp dried basil
- 1tsp dried oregano
- 2 bayleaves
- 450g/1lb wheat-free spaghetti
- salt and freshly ground black pepper

1 Finely dice the onions and carrots and crush the garlic cloves. Place in a saucepan with 2 teaspoons of olive oil and sweat the vegetables in the oil until they begin to soften.

2 Finely dice the sun-dried tomatoes and add to the pan along with the soya mince, tomato paste, stock or water and herbs. Bring to the boil and simmer for 5 minutes.

3 Place the spaghetti in a large pan of boiling water with the remaining 2 teaspoons of olive oil. Bring to the boil, simmer for 5 minutes, then drain. Add the spaghetti to the sauce and continue to cook for another 20–30 minutes, stirring occasionally until the spaghetti is soft and tender and has soaked up some of the juices from the sauce. Add more water if the sauce becomes too dry. Season with salt and black pepper, remove the bayleaves and serve. The bolognaise can be frozen.

Roasted Ratatouille with Herb Polenta

Serves 4

Other vegetables, such as swede, celery, mushroom, celeriac and aubergine (eggplant), could be used in this recipe. Carrot juice is also a useful substitute, to take the place of the tomato sauce. The herb polenta can be made up in batches and frozen, cut into rounds, for use at a later date. There's no need to defrost it, just heat from frozen on a griddle or in a frying pan.

RATATOUILLE
3 garlic cloves
4tbsp olive oil
3 large carrots
2 parsnips
1 large sweet red pepper
1 large fennel
6 medium onions
3 tomatoes
1tsp dried sage
½tsp dried thyme
12 black olives
750ml/25fl oz/3 cups water
3tbsp tomato paste

HERB POLENTA
175g/6oz/1 cup plus 3tbsp polenta flour
300ml/10fl oz/1¼ cups cold water
600ml/20fl oz/2½ cups boiling water
30g/1oz/2tbsp margarine
salt and freshly ground black pepper
1tsp dried thyme
or 1tbsp fresh thyme

1 Crush the garlic cloves, mix with the olive oil and brush some over 2 medium baking trays.
2 Cut the carrots and parsnips into large chunks, the sweet pepper and fennel into 8 sections and the onions into halves.
3 Place the vegetables on the baking trays and brush with the remaining olive oil and garlic.
4 Bake in a preheated 200°C/400°F/gas mark 6 oven for approximately 40 minutes or until the vegetables are brown and cooked. Note that if you use mushrooms or aubergine (eggplant) these will cook more quickly than the other vegetables.

5 Cut the tomatoes into quarters and place in a large saucepan with the herbs, olives, water and tomato paste. Bring to the boil, then add the roasted vegetables and mix gently. Heat through.
6 Prepare the polenta. Place the polenta and cold water in a saucepan and mix until smooth. Add the boiling water, mix well and bring to the boil, stirring. Continue to cook the polenta over a low heat, stirring regularly for approximately 5 minutes or until the mixture starts to come away from the sides of the pan.
7 Add the margarine, salt and black pepper and thyme. Mix well and allow to cool.
8 Tip the polenta on to a work surface and press out to a thickness of 1cm/½ inch. Cut into rounds using a pastry cutter.
9 Place the polenta rounds onto a greased griddle or frying pan and cook until beginning to brown on both sides. Serve with the roasted ratatouille.

Sweet Peppers Stuffed with Mushrooms and Cashew Nuts

Serves 4

Halved sweet peppers are piled high with a chunky mushroom, onion and nut sauce which browns and crisps on the surface but remains soft inside.

60g/2oz/scant ½ cup hazelnuts
125g/4oz/⅔ cup cashew nuts
3 onions
225g/8oz mushrooms
2 garlic cloves
4tsp olive oil
2tbsp rice flour
350ml/12fl oz/1½ cups passata (sieved tomatoes)
½tsp dried thyme
½tsp dried rosemary
salt and freshly ground black pepper
2 sweet red peppers
2 sweet green peppers

1. Toast the nuts in a medium oven until lightly brown. Place in a large mixing bowl.
2. Cut the onions into large dice, the mushrooms into halves or quarters and crush the garlic cloves.
3. Place the onion and 1 crushed garlic clove in a saucepan with 2 teaspoons of olive oil and sweat the onion in the oil until soft and beginning to brown. Place in the bowl with the nuts.
4. Place the chopped mushrooms in the saucepan with the remaining garlic and olive oil and sweat the mushrooms in the oil until they just begin to soften. Add to the onions and nuts in the bowl.
5. Mix the rice flour with the passata (sieved tomatoes) and place in a saucepan. Bring to the boil, stirring, and simmer for 1 minute.
6. Add the tomato mixture to the other ingredients along with the herbs. Mix well and season to taste with salt and black pepper.
7. Halve the peppers, cutting lengthways through the middle of each stalk. Leave the stalks intact, but remove the cores and seeds.
8. Place the halved sweet peppers, cut side up, on a baking tray (cover the tray with foil if you want to save on washing up). Pile the nut

mixture into the sweet peppers and cover with greased foil, tucking it in around the edges of the tray.

9 Bake in a preheated 200°C/400°F/gas mark 6 oven for approximately 50 minutes or until the peppers are soft but not mushy. Remove the foil cover for the last 10 minutes of cooking to allow the nut mixture to brown and crisp. Serve with rice or potatoes and salads.

Indian-Style Roasted Vegetables with Pilau Rice and Dahl

Serves 4

Try using other vegetables in this recipe such as fennel, parsnips, mushrooms and tomatoes. Mushrooms and tomatoes should be added half way through the cooking time to prevent over cooking.

DAHL
175g/6oz/scant 1 cup red split lentils
1tsp cumin seeds
½tsp turmeric
½tsp ground coriander
½tsp grated fresh ginger
1 garlic clove, crushed
¼tsp chilli powder
850ml/30fl oz/3¾ cups water
salt and freshly ground black pepper

ROAST VEGETABLES
2–3in piece fresh ginger
2–3 garlic cloves
1tsp ground coriander
½tsp chilli powder
¼tsp ground cardamom
¼tsp garam masala
3tbsp olive oil
salt and freshly ground black pepper
3 medium courgettes (zucchini)
2 medium carrots
2 sweet red peppers
8 small onions
1 medium aubergine (eggplant)
2tsp cumin seeds

PILAU RICE
200g/7oz/1 cup brown basmati rice
60g/2oz/heaping ⅓ cup wild rice
1 heaped tsp turmeric
60g/2oz/scant ½ cup raisins

1 Place the lentils in a saucepan with the remaining ingredients for the dahl. Bring to the boil and simmer gently for 1½ hours or until the dahl is thick and smooth. Stir occasionally.

2 Finely grate the ginger and crush the garlic cloves. Press the ginger and garlic through a fine metal sieve using the back of a spoon until you have approximately 1½ teaspoons of juice. Place this in a large bowl.
3 Add the ground coriander, chilli powder, cardamom, garam masala and olive oil and whisk until smooth. Season with salt and black pepper.
4 Cut the courgettes (zucchini) and carrots into 2.5cm/1 inch lengths, the sweet peppers into 8 pieces, the onions into halves and the aubergine (eggplant) into 1cm/½ inch slices.
5 Place the vegetables in the bowl with the olive oil and spices and toss until well coated.
6 Place the vegetables on to 2 baking trays and sprinkle with the cumin seeds.
7 Bake in a preheated 200°C/400°F/gas mark 6 oven for approximately 30 minutes or until the vegetables are browned and cooked. Turn during cooking if the vegetables are beginning to dry.
8 Meanwhile, prepare the rice. Wash the rice and place in a pan with the turmeric and 1.2 litres/40fl oz/5 cups of boiling water. Bring to the boil and simmer for 20 minutes, adding the raisins a few minutes before the end of the cooking time.
9 Sieve to remove any cooking liquid. Serve the roasted vegetables along with the pilau rice and individual bowls of dahl.

Thai Tofu with Coriander, Chilli and Ginger

Serves 4

This is a delicious mixture of vegetables and tofu in a soup-like sauce. Serve in bowls, placing each bowl on a plate along with a small pile of rice and some plain soya yogurt to accompany.

2 medium onions
2 garlic cloves
5cm/2in piece fresh ginger
1tsp sesame oil
2tsp olive oil
600ml/20fl oz/2½ cups vegetable stock
850ml/30fl oz/3¾ cups water
1tbsp lemon juice
1tsp lemon rind
2 heaped tsp Chinese five spice powder
2tbsp tomato paste
2 large kaffir lime leaves
125g/4oz/2 cups broccoli florets
60g/2oz mushrooms
1 small sweet red pepper
125g/4oz green beans *or* asparagus
2 green *or* red chillies
285g/10oz packet tofu
1tbsp finely chopped fresh mint
1tbsp finely chopped fresh coriander (cilantro)
1tbsp finely chopped fresh basil
salt and black pepper

1 Dice the onions and crush the garlic cloves. Grate half of the ginger and slice the remainder into fine slices.
2 Place the onion, garlic and ginger in a saucepan with the sesame and olive oil and sweat them until the onion begins to soften.
3 Add the stock, water, lemon juice, lemon rind, Chinese five spice powder, tomato paste and the kaffir lime leaves. Bring to the boil and simmer while preparing the vegetables.
4 Slice the mushrooms and deseed and slice the sweet pepper flesh. Cut the beans or asparagus into 2.5cm/1 inch lengths. Deseed and finely slice the chillies and cube the tofu. Add the vegetables and tofu to the pan and simmer until cooked.
5 Add the mint, coriander (cilantro) and basil. Season with salt and black pepper, remove the kaffir lime leaves and serve.

Tofu and Vegetable Kebabs with Oriental Pesto Sauce

Serves 4

MARINADE
juice of 1 orange
juice of ½ lemon
½tsp lemon rind
1tsp grated fresh ginger
1 garlic clove, crushed
1tsp chilli sauce *or* ½tsp chilli powder
1tsp sesame oil
2tbsp olive oil

KEBABS
285g/10oz packet plain tofu
3tbsp sesame seeds
2 courgettes (zucchini)
1 sweet red *or* yellow pepper
16 button mushrooms
16 cherry tomatoes
8 kebab skewers

ORIENTAL PESTO SAUCE
1 small green chilli
2tbsp chopped fresh basil
2tbsp chopped fresh coriander (cilantro)
2tbsp chopped fresh mint
1tbsp chopped fresh parsley
salt and black pepper

1. Mix together all the marinade ingredients. Cut the tofu into 16 cubes and soak the tofu cubes in the marinade for approximately 3 hours.
2. Remove the tofu from the marinade and drain, reserving the marinade. Dip each piece of tofu into the sesame seeds until well coated.
3. Cut the courgettes (zucchini) and sweet pepper into 16 pieces, then thread all the vegetables and cubes of tofu on to 8 skewers, alternating the ingredients.
4. Place the kebabs on a baking tray and brush them with the marinade. Reserve the remainder of the marinade for the pesto sauce.
5. Bake the kebabs, uncovered, in a preheated 200°C/400°F/gas mark 6 oven for 25–30 minutes or until the vegetables are cooked.
6. Meanwhile, deseed the chilli and place in a food processor with the fresh herbs, salt, pepper and the remaining marinade. Process until smooth. If you do not have a food processor, finely chop the herbs and chilli and mix with the remaining marinade. Serve the kebabs on cooked rice, accompanied by the oriental pesto sauce.

Vegetable and Tofu Stir-Fry with Sun-Dried Tomatoes and Olives

Serves 4

This quick and easy dish is somewhere between a stir-fry and a casserole, cooked on top of the stove.

- 2 onions
- 2 carrots
- 2 courgettes (zucchini)
- 125g/4oz mushrooms
- 1 garlic clove
- 1tbsp olive oil
- 285g/10oz packet plain tofu
- 12 olives
- 6 sun-dried tomatoes
- 1tbsp tomato paste
- 200ml/7fl oz/¾ cup water
- 2tbsp chopped fresh tarragon
- salt and freshly ground black pepper

1. Cut the onions into segments, the carrots into sticks, the courgettes (zucchini) into slices and the mushrooms into halves or quarters.
2. Crush the garlic clove. Place the garlic, onion and carrots in a saucepan with the olive oil and sweat the vegetables in the oil for approximately 5 minutes.
3. Add the courgettes (zucchini) and mushrooms and sweat the vegetables for a few more minutes until they begin to soften and brown.
4. Cube the tofu, halve the olives and dice the sun-dried tomatoes, and add to the pan. Mix the tomato paste with the water and add to the pan.
5. Bring to the boil, add the tarragon and simmer until the vegetables are just cooked.
6. Season to taste with salt and black pepper and serve with salads and rice, baked potatoes or wheat-free pasta.

Leek and Potato Pie

Serves 4

Mashed potatoes are combined with leeks and a creamy sauce to produce a tasty and comforting winter dish. If acceptable, sprinkle the surface with a mixture of breadcrumbs and grated cheese for a crispy topping.

1.1kg/2½lbs peeled potatoes
565g/1¼lbs leeks
2tbsp rice flour
1tsp mustard
425ml/15fl oz/2 cups soya milk
½tsp lemon rind
¼tsp grated nutmeg
1 bayleaf
15g/½oz/1tbsp vegetarian margarine
salt and freshly ground black pepper
4tbsp chopped almonds, to garnish

1. Cut the potatoes and leeks into even-sized pieces. Boil the potatoes until soft and steam the leeks until almost cooked.
2. Make a white sauce by mixing the rice flour and mustard with a little soya milk until smooth. Stir in the remaining milk along with the lemon rind, nutmeg, bayleaf and margarine. Bring to the boil, stirring constantly, and simmer for 2 minutes.
3. Drain the potatoes, place in a large bowl and mash until smooth. Remove the bayleaf from the white sauce and add the sauce to the mashed potatoes along with the leeks. Mix well and season with salt and black pepper.
4. Place the mixture in 1 large or 4 small gratin dishes. Sprinkle the surface with the chopped nuts and bake in a preheated 200°C/400°F/gas mark 6 oven for 15 minutes until the mixture is warmed through and the nuts are brown. Serve with a selection of salads. This dish freezes well.

Leek and Lentil Terrine

Serves 4

A creamy combination of leeks, fennel and cashew nuts is surrounded with a baked lentil mixture in this recipe. Celery could be substituted for the fennel if this is not available.

LENTIL MIXTURE

- 225g/8oz/heaping 1 cup split red lentils
- 750ml/25fl oz/3 cups water
- 1tsp garam masala
- ½tsp paprika
- ½tsp turmeric
- 1tsp grated fresh ginger
- 1 egg
- salt and freshly ground black pepper

LEEK MIXTURE

- 275g/10oz leeks, mainly white stems
- 175g/6oz fennel
- 1tsp grated fresh ginger
- 2tsp olive oil
- 60ml/2fl oz/¼ cup water
- 60g/2oz/scant ½ cup cashew nuts
- 90ml/3fl oz/⅓ cup soya milk
- 1tsp ground fennel seeds
- 1 egg
- salt and freshly ground black pepper

1. Place the lentils in a saucepan with the water, garam masala, paprika, turmeric and grated ginger. Cook for approximately 20 minutes or until the lentils are soft and most of the water has been absorbed. Allow to cool.
2. Finely slice the leeks and fennel, place in a saucepan with the olive oil and ginger and sweat the vegetables in the oil until they begin to soften. Add the water and simmer for 2–3 minutes or until the vegetables are soft.
3. Finely grind the cashew nuts in a food processor. Add the soya milk, ground fennel, the egg and half of the cooked vegetables and process until smooth. Return to the pan and mix with the remaining vegetables. Season with salt and black pepper.

4 To make the lentil layer, place the lentils and the egg in the food processor and process until smooth. Season with salt and black pepper.
5 Layer half of the lentil mixture in a greased and lined 900g/2lb loaf tin (pan). Carefully drop spoonfuls of the leek mixture on top of the lentils until they form another layer. Finish with another layer of lentils.
6 Bake, uncovered, in a preheated 200°C/400°F/gas mark 6 oven for 45–55 minutes or until the top is beginning to brown and the loaf is set.
7 Allow the terrine to stand for 10 minutes before turning out on to a serving dish. Serve cut into slices and accompanied by vegetables or salads.

DessertsDessertsDessertsDessert

Desserts

Stewed Nectarines with Hunza Apricots and Almond Cream

Serves 4

The combination of fresh and dried fruit in this recipe produces a really good contrast of colours, textures and flavours.

175g/6oz/scant 1 cup dried hunza apricots
600ml/20fl oz/2½ cups apple juice
6 fresh nectarines
2tbsp rosewater

1. Soak the apricots overnight in the apple juice. Place the apricots and apple juice in a saucepan, bring to the boil and simmer until the apricots are tender. The length of time required will depend on the dryness of the apricots.
2. Halve and stone (pit) the nectarines and add to the apricots along with the rosewater. Simmer for another 5 minutes or until the nectarines are just tender. Serve hot or cold with almond cream.

Almond Cream

Follow the recipe for Cashew Nut Cream (page 178) but substitute ground almonds for cashew nuts and ¼ teaspoon almond extract for the vanilla extract.

Fruit Kebabs with Spiced Pear and Tahini Dip

Serves 4

These fruit kebabs are stunning in both taste and appearance, and are a lovely way to use fruits in season.

SPICED PEAR AND TAHINI DIP
90g/3oz dried pears
425ml/15fl oz/2 cups water
1tsp ground cinnamon
3tbsp light tahini

KEBABS
Choose a selection of five fruits from the following:
4 figs, halved
1 mango, cubed
½ pineapple, cut into segments
8 fresh dates
8 large strawberries
2 bananas cut into 2.5cm/1in lengths
2 peaches, quartered
2 apricots, quartered
2 sharon fruit, quartered

8 small skewers
sunflower oil for brushing

1. Prepare the dip. Finely dice the dried pears and simmer in the water until soft, approximately 10 minutes.
2. Place the pears, cooking liquid, cinnamon and tahini in a food processor and process until smooth. Add a little more water if the mixture is too thick. If you do not have a food processor, press the cooked pears through a sieve and beat together with the remaining ingredients. Set aside.
3. Thread 5–6 pieces of fruit on to each kebab skewer, alternating colours and shapes. Place the kebabs on a baking tray.
4. Brush the fruit with sunflower oil and place under a hot grill (broiler) for 3–4 minutes on each side.
5. Serve immediately, accompanied by the spiced pear and tahini dip.

Poached Pears with Carob Sauce

Serves 4

Fried or baked bananas may be used in this recipe instead of the pears. The carob sauce is delicious poured over ice creams (see index).

4 pears
125ml/4fl oz/½ cup water
7cm/3in piece vanilla pod

CAROB SAUCE
60g/2oz/scant ½ cup dried dates
30g/1oz/¼ cup carob powder
180ml/6fl oz/scant ¾ cup water
2tbsp light tahini
½tsp vanilla extract
toasted almonds, to decorate

1. Peel the pears and cut in half lengthways. Remove the cores. Place the pears in a saucepan along with the water and vanilla pod. Cover the pan, bring the water to the boil and simmer for 10–15 minutes until the pears are tender.
2. Remove the pears from any remaining liquid and place, cut side down, on to a serving plate or plates.
3. Cut the dates into small pieces and place in a saucepan along with the carob powder and water. Bring to the boil and simmer gently until the dates have broken down and the sauce is smooth when beaten.
4. Add the tahini and vanilla extract and beat well. Add a little more water if the sauce is too thick; it should, however, be firm enough to coat each pear without running off.
5. Spoon the sauce over each individual pear. Sprinkle a few toasted almonds on the surface. Serve either warm when just cooked or chill for 1 hour in the refrigerator before serving.

Fruit Salad with Passion Fruit and Orange Sauce

Serves 4

This colourful, easily prepared fruit salad is quite impressive served with this delightful sauce.

680g/1½lb selection of fruit e.g. mango, pineapple, strawberries, kiwi fruit, orange, melon, grapes	PASSION FRUIT SAUCE 6 passion fruit 3 oranges

1. Prepare the passion fruit sauce. Halve the passion fruit and scoop out the insides into a pan. Bring to the boil and simmer for 3 minutes. Add a little orange juice if there is insufficient fruit to cover the bottom of the pan.
2. Press the passion fruit through a sieve to remove the seeds.
3. Squeeze the juice from the oranges and add this to the passion fruit juice. Stir to combine.
4. Make a fruit salad by peeling the fruit and cutting into bite-sized pieces. Mix together in a bowl.
5. Serve the fruit salad in bowls with the passion fruit sauce served separately, ready to pour over.

Fruit Salad with Cinnamon and Apple Sauce

Choose a selection of non-acidic fruit such as apple, pear, banana, peach and grapes. Cut the fruit into bite-sized pieces and mix together in a bowl. For the sauce, mix 300ml/10fl oz/1¼ cups of apple juice, 6 tablespoons light tahini and 1 teaspoon ground cinnamon in a food processor until smooth. Serve the sauce in a sauce boat or jug along with the fruit salad.

Prune and Almond Tart with Pine Nuts

Serves 4

A moist filling combines with crispy pastry in this delicious tart. No one would guess that it is wheat and sugar free. Try substituting fresh pears if dried fruit is not well tolerated but place the pears in the centre of the topping to prevent the base becoming soggy.

PASTRY BASE
30g/1oz/⅓ cup ground almonds
60g/2oz/scant ½ cup rice flour
¼tsp ground cinnamon
⅛tsp ground cloves
2tbsp water
1tbsp sunflower oil
2tbsp tahini

FILLING
60g/2oz/scant ½ cup dried dates
60ml/2fl oz/¼ cup water
60g/2oz/¼ cup vegetable margarine
125g/4oz/1⅓ cups ground almonds
2 eggs
2tbsp soya flour
½tsp almond extract
125g/4oz/scant ½ cup moist pitted prunes
15g/½oz/2tbsp pine nuts

1 Prepare the pastry. Place all the pastry ingredients in a food processor and process until the mixture forms crumbs. If you do not have a food processor, mix the dry ingredients together, then the wet ingredients and combine the mixtures with a fork. Press the crumb mixture into the base but not the sides of a 20–22cm/8–9 inch flan dish. (If you want the pastry to come up the sides of the flan dish use an extra half portion of the pastry ingredients.)
2 Bake the pastry in a preheated 200°C/400°F/gas mark 6 oven for 15 minutes or until lightly browned.
3 Meanwhile, prepare the filling. Finely dice the dates and simmer in the water until just soft. Add the margarine and allow it to soften. Add the ground almonds. Beat the eggs and add along with the soya flour and almond extract. Beat well or process until smooth.

4 Place the pitted prunes (halved if large) on the pastry base.
5 Place the almond mixture on top and smooth the surface.
6 Sprinkle with the pine nuts and bake in a preheated 190°C/375°F/ gas mark 5 oven for approximately 20–25 minutes or until golden and firm to the touch. Serve warm or cold with Vanilla Custard, Almond Cream or ice cream (see page 162). The prune and almond tart is suitable for freezing.

Pumpkin Pie

Serves 4

The non-wheat pastry base and savoury filling in this pie produce an unexpectedly delicious tart. Sweet potatoes produce a similar result and can be substituted for the pumpkin if desired.

450g/1lb pumpkin flesh
125g/4oz/scant 1 cup dried dates
125ml/4fl oz/½ cup water
2 eggs
2tbsp soya flour
60ml/2fl oz/¼ cup soya milk
½tsp vanilla extract
1tsp ground cinnamon
½tsp ground ginger
½tsp grated nutmeg
½tsp allspice
⅛tsp ground cloves

PASTRY BASE
30g/1oz/⅓ cup ground almonds
60g/2oz/6tbsp rice flour
¼tsp ground cinnamon
⅛tsp ground cloves
2tbsp water
1tbsp sunflower oil
2tbsp light tahini

1. Prepare the pastry base. Place the pastry ingredients in a food processor and process until the mixture forms crumbs. Press the crumb mixture into the base, but not the sides, of a 20–22cm/8–9 inch flan dish. If you do not have a food processor, mix the dry ingredients, then the wet ingredients and combine the two mixtures with a fork.
2. Bake the pastry case in a preheated 200°C/400°F/gas mark 6 oven for approximately 15 minutes or until it is beginning to brown around the edges.
3. Dice the pumpkin flesh (you do not need to peel the pumpkin, unless the skin is blemished or tough) and steam for approximately 15 minutes or until soft.
4. Finely chop the dates and stew in the 125ml/4fl oz/½ cup water until soft.

5 Place all the filling ingredients in the food processor and process until smooth. If you do not have a food processor, mash the pumpkin flesh until smooth, beat the eggs and combine all the ingredients, mixing well.
6 Pour the mixture on to the cooked pastry case and level the surface.
7 Place in the preheated 200°C/400°F/gas mark 6 oven for 15 minutes, then lower the temperature to 150°C/300°F/gas mark 2 and bake for another 30 minutes. Serve warm or cold with ice cream, Vanilla Custard or Cashew Nut Cream (see index). The pumpkin pie freezes well.

Apple Tarte Tatin

Serves 4

If you prefer, use stevia (see page 43) in this recipe to sweeten the apples instead of dates.

PASTRY	FILLING
30g/1oz/⅓ cup ground almonds	2 sweet apples
60g/2oz/6tbsp rice flour	30g/1oz/scant ¼ cup dried dates
¼tsp ground cinnamon	150ml/5fl oz/⅔ cup water
⅛tsp ground cloves	2 tart eating apples
2tbsp water	1tbsp sunflower oil
1tbsp sunflower oil	
2tbsp light tahini	

1 Prepare the pastry base. Place the pastry ingredients in food processor and process until the mixture forms crumbs. Press the crumb mixture into the base, but not the sides, of a 20–22cm/8–9 inch flan dish. If you do not have a food processor, mix the dry ingredients together, then the wet ingredients and combine the two mixtures with a fork.

2 Bake the pastry case in a preheated 200°C/400°F/gas mark 6 oven for approximately 15 minutes or until it is beginning to brown around the edges.

3 Peel, core and chop the sweet apples and stew with the chopped dates and water until soft. Beat well to break up the dates or process until smooth.

4 Quarter and core the tart apples but do not remove the skin. Finely slice into sections.

5 Place the stewed apple and date mixture on top of the pastry, then layer the sliced apples on top in overlapping concentric circles.

6 Brush the surface with sunflower oil and bake in the preheated 200°C/400°F/gas mark 6 oven for 15–20 minutes or until the apples are cooked and beginning to brown. Serve warm or cold with ice cream, Vanilla Custard or Cinnamon and Apple Sauce (see page 165).

Banana and Date Tarte Tatin

1 quantity pastry, page 170

FILLING

4 medium ripe bananas

1tbsp sunflower oil

1tbsp lemon juice

1tsp lemon rind

1tsp ground cinnamon

¼tsp allspice

60g/2oz/scant ½ cup fresh dates

1 Make the pastry as instructed but cook for 20 minutes or until the base is well cooked.
2 Peel and slice the bananas and fry in the sunflower oil until they begin to soften and brown.
3 Add the lemon juice, lemon rind, cinnamon and allspice and mix well. Slice the fresh dates, toss with the other ingredients and pile the mixture on top of the pastry base. Serve immediately.

Pecan Pie

Serves 4

In this recipe, the spicy pastry base is complemented by a delicious nutty filling.

1 quantity pastry, page 170	90g/3oz/scant ¾ cup dried dates
FILLING	125g/4oz/1⅓ cups ground almonds
90g/3oz carrots	¼tsp almond extract
125–150ml/4–5fl oz/½–⅔ cup water	60g/2oz/½ cup pecan nuts

1. Prepare the pastry as instructed and bake in a preheated 200°C/400°F/gas mark 6 oven for approximately 15 minutes or until beginning to brown around the edges.
2. Grate the carrots and simmer in the water for 3 minutes. Chop the dates, add to the pan and simmer until soft. The mixture should be quite moist. Add a little more water if it starts to dry out before the carrots and dates are cooked.
3. Place the ground almonds, almond extract and cooked date mixture in a food processor and process until smooth. If you do not have a food processor, mash well until the mixture is as smooth as possible.
4. Spoon the mixture on top of the pastry and level out the surface. Arrange the pecan nuts in concentric circles on top of the mixture and press lightly into the surface.
5. Bake in a preheated 200°C/400°F/gas mark 6 oven for 15–20 minutes or until the pie is beginning to brown and become firm. Serve hot or cold with ice cream, Vanilla Custard or Cinnamon and Apple Sauce (see page 165). This recipe is suitable for freezing.

Baked Banana and Coconut Cheesecake

Serves 4

This is a delicately-flavoured, creamy cheesecake on a crisp chewy base.

BASE	TOPPING
45g/1½oz/heaping ¼ cup chopped dates	125g/4oz creamed coconut
90ml/3fl oz/⅓ cup water	290g/10oz packet silken tofu
30g/1oz rice cakes *or* puffed rice cereal	250g/9oz banana flesh
45g/1½oz/½ cup desiccated (shredded) coconut	½tsp lemon rind
2tsp sunflower oil	½tsp vanilla extract

1 Prepare the base. Stew the dates in the water until soft and thick. Break the rice cakes into small pieces and process in a food processor or crush with a rolling pin until finely ground.
2 Add the desiccated (shredded) coconut, rice cakes and oil to the dates and mix. Press into the base of a 20cm/8 inch flan dish.
3 Prepare the topping. Cut up the coconut block and place in a food processor with the silken tofu, banana flesh, lemon rind and vanilla extract. Process until smooth. If you do not have a food processor, melt the coconut over a gentle heat, mash the bananas and silken tofu, then mix all the ingredients together.
4 Pour the cheesecake mixture on to the base and bake in a preheated 170°C/325°F/gas mark 3 oven for 35–45 minutes or until just set. The mixture will still be quite soft so do not overcook. It will set firmer on cooling. Serve hot or cold.

Spiced Raisin Cheesecake

Follow the above recipe adding ½ teaspoon ground cinnamon and ½ teaspoon grated nutmeg to the topping. Sprinkle 30g/1oz/¼ cup raisins over the base before pouring on the topping. Bake as before.

Hazelnut and Strawberry Tortes

Serves 4

This is a very useful recipe as the hazelnut tortes can be made in advance and kept in an airtight container for a few days. Do not assemble the tortes with the fruit until needed or they will become soggy. Try substituting almonds for the hazelnuts and other fruit for the strawberries when these are not in season. You could use peaches, mango, raspberries, sharon fruit and bananas or a mixture of dried and fresh fruit.

HAZELNUT TORTES
90g/3oz/scant ¾ cup dried dates
90ml/3fl oz/⅓ cup water
125g/4oz/¾ cup hazelnuts
3 egg whites
4tsp rice flour

FILLING
290g/10oz packet silken tofu
½tsp vanilla extract
350g/10oz strawberries plus 8 for decoration
60–90g/2–3oz/⅓–½ cup hazelnuts
Mint leaves, to decorate

1 Prepare the tortes. Finely dice the dates and stew in the water until soft – this should produce a thick purée.
2 Toast the hazelnuts in a medium oven or grill (broiler) until golden brown (toast those for the filling at the same time), then rub between finger and thumb to remove the skins. Finely grind all the hazelnuts in a food processor or using a mortar and pestle.
3 Beat the egg whites until very stiff. Gradually mix the egg whites into the date purée, being careful not to beat out the air.
4 Add all but 90g/3oz/½ cup of the ground hazelnuts and fold in, along with the rice flour, using a metal spoon in a figure of eight movement.
5 Place the mixture in eight mounds on 2 greased baking trays. Spread each mound into a 7cm/3 inch circle approximately 8mm/⅓ inch thick.
6 Bake in a preheated 170°C/325°F/gas mark 3 oven for 10–15 minutes or until well browned and set. Allow the tortes to cool.

7 Meanwhile, make the filling. Beat or process the silken tofu with the vanilla extract until smooth.
8 Finely dice the strawberries and add to the tofu, mixing to combine.
9 Add sufficient toasted ground hazelnuts to stiffen the mixture so that it will hold its shape.
10 Place a hazelnut torte on each of the serving plates. Divide two-thirds of the strawberry mixture between the tortes and spread out to cover the surface of each torte. Place another torte on top, then spoon the remaining strawberry mixture on the top of each torte in the centre.
11 Decorate the top of each torte with a strawberry cut in half and mint leaves. Press quartered strawberries into the filling where it oozes out between the tortes. Serve at once.

Peach Choux Pudding

Serves 4

Corn flour is very finely ground maize. It is different from the cornflour (cornstarch) sold in supermarkets, as it hasn't been bleached and retains its yellow colour.

4 medium peaches	90ml/3fl oz/⅓ cup cold water
	200ml/7fl oz/¾ cup boiling water
TOPPING	15g/½oz/1tbsp margarine
60g/2oz/6tbsp unbleached corn flour (cornstarch)	½tsp vanilla extract
	2 eggs, beaten

1. Halve and stone (pit) the peaches. Slice a small piece from the rounded side of each peach so that they stand firmly, stone side uppermost, in a baking dish.
2. Place the corn flour (cornstarch) in a pan and mix in the cold water. Add the boiling water and stir well. Add the margarine and vanilla extract, bring to the boil and simmer over a low heat, stirring constantly, for 2 minutes. The mixture should be thick and smooth. Allow to cool slightly.
3. Gradually beat the eggs into the mixture, a little at a time, using a wooden spoon. Place spoonfuls of the mixture on top of each half peach.
4. Bake in a preheated 425°F/220°C/gas mark 7 oven for approximately 15 minutes or until well risen and golden brown.
5. Serve immediately with ice cream or Vanilla Custard (see index).

VARIATIONS

Substitute plums, apricots or nectarines in the above recipe or place spoonfuls of the mixture on top of stewed fruit such as apple and blackberry or rhubarb and date. Another option is to cook the mixture in bun tins (muffin pans) with 2–3 pitted prunes or soft dried apricots in the centre of each.

Sweet Potato Pudding

Serves 4

This unusual pudding is really easy to make and quite delicious.

680g/1½lb sweet potatoes
60g/2oz creamed coconut
600ml/20fl oz/2½ cups soya milk
½tsp vanilla extract
½tsp grated nutmeg
1tsp ground cinnamon
½tsp ground cardamom
60g/2oz/scant ½ cup raisins, optional

1 Peel and roughly chop the sweet potatoes. Chop the creamed coconut.
2 Place the potatoes and coconut in a food processor and process until finely chopped. Add the soya milk, vanilla extract, nutmeg, cinnamon and cardamom and process again until quite smooth. If you do not have a food processor, finely grate the sweet potatoes and dissolve the creamed coconut in some warm soya milk. Combine all the ingredients.
3 Add the raisins and place in a well greased baking dish.
4 Bake in a preheated 150°C/300°F/gas mark 2 oven for approximately 1 hour or until set and beginning to brown on top. Serve warm.

Caribbean Cobbler with Cashew Nut Cream

Serves 4

2 large mangoes
2 large firm bananas
3–4 wrinkled passion fruit
grated rind of ½ orange
juice of ½ orange

SCONE TOPPING
125g/4oz/¾ cup plus 2tbsp rice flour
125g/4oz/¾ cup plus 2tbsp potato flour
2tsp baking powder
30g/1oz/2tbsp margarine
1 egg made up to 180ml/6fl oz/scant ¾ cup with soya milk

CASHEW NUT CREAM
90g/3oz/heaping ½ cup cashew nuts
150g/5oz silken tofu
½tsp vanilla extract
2tbsp soya milk

1 Peel and stone (pit) the mangoes and cut the flesh into large chunks.
2 Slice the bananas into 2.5cm/1 inch pieces.
3 Halve the passion fruit and scoop out the seeds.
4 Combine the mango flesh, sliced banana, passion fruit seeds and grated orange rind. Place in a deep-sided baking dish and pour over the orange juice.
5 Place the flours, baking powder and margarine in a food processor and process. Beat the egg and the soya milk mixture and add to the processor. Process until the mixture forms quite a soft dough. If you do not have a food processor, rub the margarine into the flours and baking powder, then mix in the egg and milk.
6 Place even-sized spoonfuls of the scone topping on to the fruit base. Do not level the surface but leave the topping in mounds.

7 Bake in a preheated 240°C/475°F/gas mark 9 oven for 10–12 minutes or until the fruit is bubbling and the topping is firm and beginning to brown. Do not overcook or the fruit will begin to break up.
8 Meanwhile, prepare the cashew nut cream. Place the cashew nuts in a food processor and process until finely ground.
9 Add the silken tofu, vanilla extract and soya milk to the ground cashews and process until smooth and creamy. Add more soya milk if you prefer a more runny cream. If you do not have a food processor, use ground almonds instead of the cashew nuts and beat the ingredients together. Serve the cobbler hot, accompanied by the cashew nut cream.

Plum, Banana, Raisin and Ginger Cobbler

Serves 4

Because there is no sugar in the topping, the fruit needs to be ripe and sweet. Alternatively, sweeten the topping with ⅛ teaspoon of stevia.

565g/1¼lb very ripe plums
2 large firm bananas
30g/1oz/scant ¼ cup raisins
1 heaped tsp grated fresh ginger
4tbsp water

SCONE TOPPING
125g/4oz/¾ cup plus 2tbsp rice flour
125g/4oz/¾ cup plus 2tbsp potato flour
2tsp baking powder
30g/1oz/2tbsp margarine
1 egg made up to 180ml/6fl oz/scant ¾ cup with soya milk

1 Scald the plums for 30 seconds in boiling water, then peel. This makes the plums sweeter as it is the skins which tend to taste sharp. Cut the plums into halves or quarters and remove the stones.
2 Cut the bananas into 2.5cm/1inch pieces.
3 Mix together the plums, bananas, raisins and grated ginger and place in a deep-sided dish. Pour the water over the fruit.
4 Place the flours, baking powder and margarine in a food processor and process. Beat the egg and the soya milk mixture and add to the processor. Process until the mixture forms quite a soft dough. If you do not have a food processor, rub the margarine into the flours and baking powder then mix in the egg and milk.
5 Place even-sized spoonfuls of the scone topping on to the fruit base. Do not level the surface but leave the topping in mounds.
6 Bake in a preheated 240°C/475°F/gas mark 9 oven for 10–12 minutes or until the fruit is bubbling and the topping is firm and beginning to brown. Do not overcook or the fruit will begin to break up. Serve hot with Cashew Nut Cream, Cinnamon and Apple Sauce or Vanilla Custard (see index).

Spiced Apple Sponge with Vanilla Custard

Serves 4

I have used stevia (see page 43) in this recipe to sweeten both the sponge and the custard. If you do not want to use stevia, use 60g/2oz/scant ½ cup chopped dates stewed in 60ml/2fl oz/¼ cup water in the sponge and 2tbsp dates stewed in 60ml/2fl oz/¼ cup water in the custard.

3 tart eating apples
½tsp grated nutmeg
½tsp ground cinnamon
½tsp ground cloves
2tbsp water

SPONGE
125g/4oz stewed apple
90ml/3fl oz sunflower oil
60g/2oz/6tbsp rice flour
30g/1oz/3tbsp soya flour
60g/2oz/6tbsp potato flour
1 heaped tsp mixed spice
1tbsp molasses, optional
2 eggs
1tbsp baking powder
⅛tsp stevia

VANILLA CUSTARD
600ml/20fl oz/2½ cups soya milk
⅛tsp stevia
4tbsp unbleached corn flour (cornstarch)
1tsp vanilla extract

1. Peel and slice the apples and simmer with the nutmeg, cinnamon, cloves and water until soft. Place in a shallow baking dish.
2. Place all the sponge ingredients in a food processor and process until smooth, adding a little water if necessary to obtain a soft dropping consistency. If you do not have a food processor, beat the eggs and then beat in the remaining ingredients.
3. Place the sponge mixture on top of the apples and smooth the surface.
4. Bake in a preheated 200°C/400°F/gas mark 6 oven for approximately 25 minutes or until the sponge is cooked and brown.
5. Meanwhile, prepare the vanilla custard. Place all the ingredients into a pan and beat to blend in the corn flour (cornstarch).
6. Bring to the boil, stirring constantly, and simmer for 2 minutes. Serve the sponge and custard warm.

Banana and Almond Cream Dessert

Serves 4

This is a really quick and easy dessert to make from ingredients that can be kept in stock and used for unexpected guests.

90g/3oz/⅓ cup ground almonds
290g/10oz packet silken tofu
4 medium bananas
1tsp ground cinnamon
½tsp almond extract
2tbsp light tahini
2tbsp split almonds

1. Place all the ingredients, except the almonds, in a food processor and process until smooth. If you do not have a processor mash the bananas, then beat in the remaining ingredients until smooth. Divide the mixture between 4 sundae glasses.
2. Toast the almonds in a medium oven or grill (broiler). Allow them to cool, then sprinkle over the banana and almond cream. Chill before serving.

Rhubarb and Ginger Fool

Serves 4

Stevia (see page 43) could be used to sweeten this dish instead of dates; simply stew the rhubarb and ginger in 2 tablespoons of water, instead of 60ml/2fl oz/¼ cup, and add ¼tsp of stevia instead of the dates.

- 450g/1lb rhubarb
- 90g/3oz/scant ¾ cup dried dates
- 1tsp grated fresh ginger
- 60ml/2fl oz/¼ cup water
- 290g/10oz packet silken tofu
- toasted almonds and mint leaves, to decorate

1. Slice the rhubarb into 2.5cm/1 inch lengths and place in a saucepan of boiling water. Simmer for 1 minute, then strain. This takes away a little of the tartness and acidity from the rhubarb.
2. Finely chop the dates and place in a saucepan with the rhubarb, grated ginger and the water. Bring to the boil and simmer until the rhubarb and dates are soft. Allow the mixture to cool.
3. Place the rhubarb mixture and the silken tofu in a food processor and process until smooth. If you do not have a food processor, beat the tofu well with a wooden spoon, then beat in the rhubarb mixture.
4. Divide the rhubarb fool between 4 individual sundae dishes and decorate with toasted almonds and mint leaves. Chill before serving.

Banana and Passion Fruit Fool

Serves 4

The passion fruit and bananas complement each other wonderfully in this quick and easy recipe.

6 passion fruit	290g/10oz packet silken tofu
60ml/2fl oz/¼ cup water	2tbsp desiccated (shredded) coconut
4 medium bananas	

1. Halve the passion fruit and scoop out the centres into a pan. Add the water, bring to the boil and simmer for 3 minutes. Press the passion fruit through a sieve to remove the seeds.
2. Place the passion fruit purée, the bananas and the silken tofu in a food processor and process until smooth. If you do not have a food processor, mash the bananas and beat well with the remaining ingredients until the mixture is smooth.
3. Divide the fool between 4 individual sundae glasses.
4. Toast the desiccated (shredded) coconut under the grill (broiler) until golden brown, then sprinkle over the surface of the fruit fools. Chill before serving.

Cashew Nut and Coconut Ice Cream

Serves 4

I like to keep ready-frozen ingredients in the freezer so that a delicious dessert can be made at a moment's notice. Soya cream can be used instead of coconut milk, provided its ingredients are acceptable.

3tbsp unbleached corn flour (cornstarch)
425ml/15fl oz/2 cups soya milk
90g/3oz/scant ¾ cup dried chopped dates
or ¼tsp stevia, see page 43
1tsp vanilla extract
125g/4oz/¾ cup cashew nuts
240ml/8fl oz/1 cup coconut milk

1 Place the corn flour (cornstarch) in a saucepan with the soya milk, chopped dates or stevia powder and vanilla extract. Mix well until the corn flour (cornstarch) is blended. Bring to the boil, stirring constantly and simmer for 2 minutes. Cover with a lid and allow to cool.
2 Pour the custard mixture into an ice cube tray or trays and freeze.
3 Place the cashew nuts in a food processor and process until finely ground, then add 90ml/3fl oz/⅓ cup coconut milk and process again. Place this mixture in an ice cube tray and freeze.
4 To assemble the ice cream, place the frozen custard cubes and the frozen coconut and cashew nut cubes in a food processor along with the remaining 150ml/5fl oz/⅔ cup of coconut milk.
5 Cover the processor with a tea towel to prevent splashes, and process until smooth. You will need to lift the lid off the processor and use a spatula to help combine the ingredients if they are not processing smoothly. Serve at once in individual sundae glasses.

Banana and Vanilla Ice Cream

Follow the above recipe, substituting 225g/8oz sliced frozen bananas for the processed cashews nuts and the coconut milk. Use 150ml/5fl oz/⅔ cup soya milk, or soya cream (if the ingredients are acceptable), to combine the ingredients instead of the coconut milk.

Carob, Coconut and Banana Ice Cream

Serves 4

This is a really easy way to make a luscious ice cream. No one will believe that it is sugar free. I like to keep ingredients ready-frozen, so that I can make this dessert at a moment's notice.

225g/8oz peeled bananas
60g/2oz/scant ½ cup dried dates
30g/1oz carob powder
180ml/6fl oz/scant ¾ cup water
½tsp vanilla extract
240ml/8fl oz/1 cup coconut milk

1. Slice the bananas, place on a baking tray and freeze until solid.
2. Finely dice the dates and place in a saucepan with the carob powder, water and vanilla extract. Simmer gently until the dates have broken down and the sauce is smooth.
3. Allow the sauce to cool and mix in 125ml/4fl oz/½ cup of coconut milk. Pour the mixture into an ice cube tray and freeze. Place the remaining coconut milk in the refrigerator to cool.
4. Place the coconut milk in a food processor along with the frozen carob cubes and frozen banana pieces.
5. Cover the processor with a tea towel to prevent splashes and process on full power until the ice cream is smooth. You may need to lift the lid off the processor and use a spatula to help combine the ingredients if not processing smoothly. Serve at once.

Strawberry and Coconut Ice Cream

Serves 4

Try to find a thick, creamy coconut milk for this recipe, as they do vary in thickness depending on the make. A watery coconut milk will produce more of a sorbet than a rich strawberry ice cream. Alternatively, you could substitute coconut cream or soya cream if the ingredients in these are acceptable.

450g/1lb strawberries	450ml/16fl oz/good 2 cups thick coconut milk

1 Halve the strawberries, place on a baking tray and freeze uncovered. Place the coconut milk in the refrigerator until very cold.
2 Place the coconut milk in a food processor. It is a good idea to wrap a tea towel round the processor to prevent splashing when the strawberries are added.
3 Switch the processor on and feed the frozen strawberries in through the funnel. Process the mixture until smooth. You will need to remove the lid from the processor and use a spatula to help combine the ingredients if they are not processing smoothly. Serve immediately.

Peach and Passion Fruit Sorbet

Serves 4

Freeze the peach flesh well in advance so that you can make up this sorbet at a moment's notice.

5–6 ripe peaches (500g/18oz peach flesh)	6 passion fruit

1 Peel and stone (pit) the peaches and cut the flesh into small chunks. Place the chunks on a baking tray and freeze until solid.
2 Halve the passion fruit and scoop out the centres into a pan. Add 60ml/2fl oz/¼ cup water, bring to the boil and simmer for 3 minutes.
3 Press the passion fruit through a sieve to remove the seeds. Make the juice up to 150ml/5fl oz/⅔ cup with water. Place the passion fruit juice in the refrigerator until cold. The passion fruit juice could be frozen if you are not making the sorbet straightaway but it will need defrosting before the next stage.
4 Place the frozen peach chunks and the passion fruit juice in a food processor and process until smooth. You may need to lift the lid off the processor at intervals and use a spatula to help combine the ingredients if they are not processing smoothly. Serve at once.

Mango and Orange Sorbet

Serves 4

Freeze the mango flesh well in advance so that you can make up this sorbet at a moment's notice.

2 large mangoes (500g/18oz mango flesh)	150ml/5fl oz/⅔ cup orange juice

1 Peel and stone (pit) the mangoes and dice the flesh. Place the diced mango on a baking tray and freeze until solid. Place the orange juice in the refrigerator to cool.

2 Place the diced mango and the orange juice in a food processor and process until smooth. You may need to lift the lid off the processor at intervals and use a spatula to help combine the ingredients if they are not processing smoothly. Serve at once.

BakingBakingBakingBakingBakin

kingBakingBakingBaking Baking

Apricot, Carrot and Polenta Cake

This is one of my favourite cakes. The polenta keeps it moist and gives it an unusual texture, while the flavour is quite delightful. Sweet potatoes can be used instead of the carrots, if preferred, and 125ml/4fl oz/½ cup of vegetable oil, such as sunflower oil, instead of the margarine.

125g/4oz carrots
125g/4oz/scant ½ cup dried apricots
90ml/3fl oz/⅓ cup orange juice
125g/4oz/½ cup vegetarian margarine
1tsp orange zest
½tsp lemon zest
150g/5oz/1 cup polenta flour
90g/3oz/9 tablespoons rice flour
3 eggs, beaten
4tsp baking powder
½tsp vanilla extract
berry fruits to garnish, optional

1 Slice the carrots and boil until soft. Weigh out 125g/4oz of carrots after cooking.
2 Dice the dried apricots and simmer in the orange juice until soft. Allow the mixture to cool.
3 Place the apricots, orange juice and carrots in a food processor and process until smooth. If you do not have a food processor, mash the ingredients well or press them through a sieve.
4 Add the margarine and mix until melted.
5 Add the orange and lemon zest, polenta, rice flour, eggs, baking powder and vanilla extract. Process or beat until smooth, adding a little extra water if needed until a soft dropping consistency is obtained.
6 Place in a greased and lined 20cm/8 inch round sponge tin (cake pan), or a 900g/2lb loaf tin (pan). Level the surface.
7 Bake in a preheated 180°C/350°F/gas mark 4 oven for 30–40 minutes or until golden brown and firm to touch.
8 Allow the cake to stand for 5 minutes then take out of the tin (pan), remove the lining paper and cool on a wire tray. Eat within 3 days or freeze in slices.
9 Garnish with berry fruits as desired.

Jamaican Banana Bread

Polenta gives this moist cake its unusual texture. Omit the raisins if they're not acceptable and a pleasant though less sweet cake will still be produced. It is delicious served sliced and buttered when cool.

225g/8oz peeled bananas
125ml/4fl oz/½ cup water
1 egg or egg replacer
60ml/2fl oz/¼ cup sunflower oil
90g/3oz/9tbsp rice flour
90g/3oz/9tbsp polenta flour
60g/2oz/6tbsp potato flour
4tsp baking powder
1 heaped tsp ground cinnamon
½tsp allspice
½tsp grated nutmeg
60g/2oz/⅔ cup walnuts
90g/3oz/scant ½ cup raisins

1 Place the bananas, water, egg and oil in a food processor and process until smooth. Add the flours, baking powder and spices and process again. If you do not have a food processor, mash the bananas until smooth, then mix in the water, beaten egg, sunflower oil, flours, baking powder and spices.
2 Break the walnuts into small pieces and add to the mixture along with the raisins. Mix in. If using a food processor, process for 10 seconds until the walnuts and raisins are mixed in but not broken up.
3 Place the mixture in a greased and lined 450g/1lb loaf tin (pan). Bake in a preheated 170°C/325°F/gas mark 3 oven for 45 minutes or until brown on top and firm to the touch.
4 Cool for 5 minutes in the tin (pan), then turn out on to a wire tray and remove the lining paper. Eat within 3 days or freeze.

Feel Good Cake

Phyto-oestrogens are food constituents which assist in hormone balancing. In Eastern countries where soya products form a large part of people's diet, women have very few problems with pre-menstrual syndrome or the menopause. In this cake I have tried to include as many of the phytonutrients as possible in order to produce a cake which has a 'feel good' factor. Try it and see. Even if you do not have hormone-related problems it is still a delicious cake that is full of natural goodness.

125g/4oz carrots
270ml/9fl oz/scant 1¼ cups water
3 star anise
3tbsp linseeds
270ml/9fl oz/scant 1¼ cups soya milk
125ml/4fl oz/½ cup soya oil
90g/3oz/9tbsp rice flour
90g/3oz/9tbsp soya flour
90g/3oz/9tbsp unbleached corn flour (cornstarch)
1tsp ground cinnamon
2tsp ground liquorice
1tsp fennel seeds
60g/2oz/heaping ½ cup almonds
30g/1oz dried apple
60g/2oz/½ cup pumpkin seeds
30g/1oz/¼ cup sunflower seeds
225g/8oz/heaping 1½ cups mixed dried fruit e.g. sultanas (golden raisins), raisins, currants
1tbsp sunflower seeds, to decorate

1 Slice the carrot and cook in the water along with the star anise, until the carrots are nearly cooked. Add the linseeds and continue to simmer for approximately 5 minutes, until the mixture is quite thick. Remove the star anise.
2 Place the carrot and linseed mixture in a food processor and process until smooth. Mash if you do not have a food processor.
3 Add the soya milk and oil, the rice, soya and corn flours and the cinnamon, liquorice and fennel seeds. Process or beat the mixture until smooth. Place the mixture in a large bowl.
4 Finely chop the almonds and dried apple and add to the cake mixture along with the pumpkin seeds, sunflower seeds and dried fruit. Mix well.

5 Place in a greased and lined 20cm/8 inch round sponge tin (cake pan) or 900g/2lb loaf tin (pan). Sprinkle the surface with sunflower seeds and press these into the cake. Bake in a preheated 170°C/325°F/gas mark 3 oven for 45 minutes, then reduce the temperature to 145°C/290°F/gas mark 1 and bake for another 30 minutes.
6 Cool for 5 minutes in the tin (pan) then turn out on to a cooling tray, remove the lining paper and allow the cake to cool. Eat within 3 days or slice and freeze.

Sweet Potato and Almond Cake

Beaten egg whites are used to make this cake light, while the ground almonds produce a moist texture and a wonderful flavour.

- 125g/4oz sweet potato
- 90g/3oz dried pears
- 125ml/4fl oz/½ cup boiling water
- 3 large eggs
- 1tsp almond extract
- 2tsp baking powder
- 90g/3oz/1 cup ground almonds
- 90g/3oz/9tbsp rice flour

1. Finely dice the sweet potato and dried pears and place in a pan with the boiling water. Simmer, covered, for approximately 10 minutes or until the pears and sweet potato are soft and most of the water has been absorbed. Allow the mixture to cool.
2. Separate the eggs, placing the whites in a large bowl. Whisk the egg whites until quite stiff.
3. Place the sweet potato, dried pears, egg yolks and almond extract in a food processor and process. If you do not have a food processor, press the mixture through a sieve.
4. Fold the mixture into the egg whites using a metal spoon in a figure of eight movement. Be gentle, to prevent the air being beaten out of the egg whites.
5. Mix the baking powder with the ground almonds and rice flour and fold this into the egg white mixture, again mixing gently, in a figure of eight movement.
6. Place the cake mixture in a greased and lined 450g/1lb loaf tin (pan) and bake in a preheated 170°C/325°F/gas mark 3 oven for 30–40 minutes or until golden brown and firm to touch.
7. Allow the cake to cool for 5 minutes in the tin (pan) before turning out to cool on a wire tray. Eat within 3 days or freeze in slices.

Date and Walnut Loaf

Polenta, together with apple, produces a moist and unusually textured cake that makes a tasty tea time treat when served sliced and buttered. Carrot or sweet potato may be substituted for the apple.

225g/8oz peeled and cored eating apple
125ml/4fl oz/½ cup water
1 egg or egg replacer
90g/3oz/9tbsp rice flour
90g/3oz/9tbsp polenta flour
60g/2oz/6tbsp potato flour
4tsp baking powder
1 heaped tsp mixed spice
60ml/2fl oz/¼ cup sunflower oil
125g/4oz/scant 1 cup dried dates
60g/2oz/⅔ cup walnuts

1. Cut the apple into thin slices and simmer gently in the water until soft. Allow the apple to cool.
2. Cut the dates and walnuts into small pieces.
3. Place the apple and its cooking liquid in a food processor together with the egg, flours, baking powder, mixed spice and sunflower oil. Process until smooth. If you do not have a food processor, mash the apple until smooth, then mix in the egg (beaten if using), flours, baking powder, spice and oil.
4. Add the dates and walnuts to the cake mixture and process or mix for a few seconds until combined. Do not break up the walnuts and dates.
5. Place the mixture in a greased and lined 450g/1lb loaf tin (pan).
6. Bake in a preheated 170°C/325°F/gas mark 3 oven for approximately 45 minutes or until firm to the touch and beginning to brown.
7. Allow the cake to cool for 5 minutes in the tin (pan). Turn out on to a wire tray and remove the lining paper. Serve sliced and buttered when cold. Eat within 3 days or freeze.

Pineapple, Orange and Ginger Cake

This is a moist fruit cake with an interesting combination of textures and flavours. If you prefer, use 125ml/4fl oz/½ cup of a vegetable oil, such as sunflower oil, instead of the margarine.

150g/5oz/1 cup dried dates
peel from 1 orange
juice from 1 orange
125g/4oz/½ cup vegetable margarine
60g/2oz/6tbsp rice flour
90g/3oz/9tbsp soya flour
60g/2oz unbleached corn flour (cornstarch)
30g/1oz/⅓ cup ground almonds
1tsp ground ginger
4tsp baking powder
3 eggs or egg replacer
125g/8oz can pineapple chunks
30g/1oz/scant ¼ cup raisins

1 Finely dice the dates and the orange peel. Make the orange juice up to 200ml/7fl oz/¾ cup with water and place in a pan with the dates and orange peel. Simmer gently until the peel is soft, the dates are soft and the mixture is beginning to solidify.
2 Beat the margarine and date mixture together using a wooden spoon or the plastic blade in a food processor (a metal blade would disintegrate the orange rind).
3 Mix the flours with the ground almonds, ginger and baking powder. Beat the eggs. If mixing by hand, add the flours and eggs gradually to the margarine and date mixture, beating between each addition. If using a food processor, add both together and process to combine.
4 Drain the pineapple and finely dice the flesh. Add the pineapple flesh and raisins to the cake mixture and mix using a wooden spoon. The mixture should have a soft dropping consistency. Add a little more liquid if it is too dry.
5 Place the mixture in a greased and lined 18cm/7 inch sponge tin (cake pan) and bake in a preheated 170°C/325°F/gas mark 3 oven for 30 minutes, then lower the temperature to 140°C/275°F/gas mark 1 and bake for another 45 minutes.

6 Allow the cake to cool for 10 minutes in the tin (pan), then turn out onto a wire tray and remove the lining paper. Eat within 3 days or freeze in slices.

Gingerbread Cake

I have used stevia (see page 43) to sweeten this cake, but if you don't want to use it substitute 90g/3oz/scant ¾ cup chopped dates stewed in 90ml/3fl oz/⅓ cup water and omit the stevia and ground almonds. Molasses is the product left when sugar is produced from sugar cane. It does contain a little sugar, but gives a wonderful flavour to this cake and is full of minerals. Substitute 1 tablespoon tahini if you do not want to use molasses.

90g/3oz/9tbsp rice flour
90g/3oz/9tbsp millet flour
60g/2oz/⅔ cup ground almonds
1tbsp molasses
2 eggs
1 heaped tsp ground cinnamon
2 heaped tsp ground ginger
½tsp allspice
90ml/3fl oz/⅓ cup sunflower oil
¼tsp stevia powder
4tsp baking powder
60–90ml/2–3fl oz/¼–⅓ cup water

1. Place all the ingredients including 60ml/2fl oz/¼ cup of the water in a food processor and process until well mixed. Add the remaining water if necessary to obtain a soft dropping consistency. If you do not have a food processor, beat all the wet ingredients together and combine the dry ingredients, then beat the two mixtures together until well blended.
2. Place the mixture in a greased and lined 450g/1lb loaf tin (pan) and bake in a preheated 180°C/350°F/gas mark 4 oven for 35–45 minutes or until firm to the touch.
3. Cool for 5 minutes in the tin (pan), then turn out on to a wire tray and remove the lining paper. Eat within 3 days or freeze in slices.

Lemon and Poppy Seed Cake

This unusual cake is flavoured with pieces of lemon rind as well as the juice. If preferred, oranges could be substituted for the lemons. I have used stevia (see page 43) to sweeten the cake but if you don't want to use it substitute 90g/3oz/scant ¾ cup chopped dates stewed in 90ml/3fl oz/⅓ cup water and omit the stevia and ground almonds.

- 2 lemons
- 2tbsp water
- 90g/3oz/9tbsp rice flour
- 90g/3oz/9tbsp millet flour
- 60g/2oz/⅔ cup ground almonds
- 1tbsp tahini
- 2 eggs
- 30g/1oz/¼ cup poppy seeds
- 1tsp vanilla extract
- 60ml/2fl oz/¼ cup lemon juice
- 90ml/3fl oz/1⅓ cup sunflower oil
- ¼tsp stevia powder
- 4tsp baking powder

1. Grate the rind from one lemon and squeeze the juice from both. Measure out 60ml/2fl oz/¼ cup of the squeezed lemon juice. Remove the pith from the second lemon skin and cut the skin into fine dice. Gently simmer the diced lemon rind in the 2 tablespoons of water for approximately 5 minutes or until the rind is soft and the water has evaporated.
2. Place the grated lemon rind, the cooked lemon rind and the lemon juice in a food processor and process until smooth using a plastic blade. If the processor does not have a plastic blade, mix in the cooked lemon rind by hand afterwards.
3. Place the mixture in a greased and lined 450g/1lb loaf tin (pan) and bake in a preheated 180°C/350°F/gas mark 4 oven for 35–45 minutes or until firm to touch and brown.
4. Cool for 5 minutes in the tin (pan), then turn out on to a wire tray and remove the lining paper. Eat within 3 days or freeze in slices.

Mango, Apricot and Orange Muffins

Makes 12

This recipe produces light, cake-textured muffins packed full of fruit and flavour. They can easily be adapted to take advantage of seasonal fruit.

- 90g/3oz carrots
- 225g/8oz fresh mango
- 90g/3oz/scant ½ cup dried apricots
- 225g/8oz/1 cup plus 9tbsp rice flour
- 240ml/8fl oz/1 cup soya milk
- 2 eggs
- 4tsp baking powder
- 2tbsp sunflower oil
- 2tsp grated orange peel

1. Slice the carrots and boil until soft. Weigh out 90g/3oz of carrots after cooking then mash or process to form a smooth purée.
2. Dice the mango flesh into 1cm/½ inch pieces and the dried apricots in to 5mm/¼ inch pieces. Dry the mango flesh on a tea towel.
3. Place the rice flour, soya milk, eggs, baking powder, sunflower oil and carrot purée in a food processor and process until smooth. If you do not have a food processor, beat the eggs then mix in the remaining ingredients.
4. Add the mango, apricot and grated orange rind, and mix in by hand or with a plastic processor blade.
5. Place the mixture in a greased muffin or bun tray, dividing it into 12 muffins and piling each high.
6. Bake in a preheated 200°C/400°F/gas mark 6 oven for 15–20 minutes, until risen and golden brown and firm to the touch.
7. Cool on a wire tray. Eat within 3 days or freeze.

VARIATIONS

Pineapple, Prune and Lemon Muffins

Substitute pineapple for the mango, prunes for the apricots and lemon rind for the orange rind. Use 90g/3oz fairly dry stewed apple instead of the carrot purée.

Blackcurrant and Apple Muffins

Substitute blackcurrants for the mango, dried apple for the apricot and 1 teaspoon vanilla extract for the orange rind. Use 90g/3oz fairly dry stewed apple instead of the carrot purée.

Banana, Cinnamon and Apricot Muffins

Substitute banana for the mango, 2 teaspoon ground cinnamon and ½ teaspoon vanilla extract for the orange rind and use 90g/3oz mashed banana instead of the carrot purée.

Pecan, Cinnamon and Raisin Muffins

Substitute 125g/4oz/scant 1 cup raisins and 125g/4oz/1 cup pecan nuts for the mango and apricots, 2 teaspoons ground cinnamon and ½ teaspoon almond extract for the orange rind and use 90g/3oz carrot purée as before.

Farmhouse Fruit Cake

No one will believe that this rich, moist fruit cake is free from sugar and wheat. It is full of natural goodness and one of my family favourites. If you prefer, 125ml/4fl oz/½ cup of oil, such as sunflower oil, may be used to replace the margarine.

- 175g/6oz/scant 1¼ cups dried dates
- 150ml/5fl oz/⅔ cup water
- 125g/4oz/½ cup vegetarian margarine
- 30g/1oz/⅓ cup ground almonds
- 1tsp ground mixed spice
- 3 eggs *or* egg replacer
- juice of 1 orange
- zest of 1 orange
- 60g/2oz/6tbsp rice flour
- 60g/2oz/6tbsp unbleached corn flour (cornstarch)
- 60g/2oz/6tbsp soya flour
- 2tsp baking powder
- 60g/2oz/⅔ cup walnuts
- 225g/8oz/heaping 1½ cups raisins
- 125g/4oz/⅔ cup grated carrot
- 1 apple, grated

1. Cut the dates into small pieces and place in a pan with the water. Simmer over a low heat for approximately 10 minutes or until the dates are soft. Allow the dates to cool.
2. Place the dates, margarine, ground almonds, mixed spice, eggs, orange juice and zest, the flours and the baking powder in a food processor and process, or beat by hand, until well blended.
3. Add the walnuts, raisins, grated carrot and grated apple and stir in by hand.
4. Place in a greased and lined 18–20cm/6–8 inch round sponge tin (cake pan) and bake in a preheated 170°C/325°F/gas mark 3 oven for 30 minutes, then lower the temperature to 140°C/275°F/gas mark 1 and bake for another 45 minutes.
5. Allow the cake to cool for 10 minutes in the tin (pan), then turn out on to a wire tray and remove the lining paper. Eat within 4 days or freeze in slices.

Apricot and Walnut Clusters

The variations on these clusters are endless. Substitute cashews, almonds or hazelnuts for the walnuts, and figs, dates or dried pears for the apricots. Oat flakes could be used instead of millet flakes, broken rice cakes instead of the rice cereal and carrot or banana purée instead of the stewed apple.

90g/3oz/scant ½ cup dried apricots
90g/3oz/1 cup walnuts
125g/4oz millet flakes
60g/2oz/⅔ cup desiccated (shredded) coconut
60g/2oz puffed rice cereal
200g/7oz peeled eating apple
60ml/2fl oz/¼ cup water
75ml/2½fl oz/5tbsp sunflower oil
1tsp ground mixed spice
½tsp vanilla extract

1. Finely dice the apricots and break the walnuts into small pieces. Place in a bowl along with the millet flakes, desiccated (shredded) coconut and puffed rice cereal.
2. Dice the apple and stew in the water until the apple is well cooked and the excess moisture has evaporated.
3. Place the apple, oil, mixed spice and vanilla extract in a food processor and process. If you do not have a food processor, mash the apple, then mix in the other ingredients.
4. Add the processed apple mixture to the dry ingredients and combine well using a wooden spoon.
5. Using your hands, form the mixture into balls about the size of a golf ball, pressing the mixture together firmly.
6. Place the clusters on a greased baking tray and bake in a preheated 180°C/350°F/gas mark 4 oven for 15–20 minutes or until golden brown and crisp on the outside. Cool on a wire tray and eat within 3 days or freeze.

Carob-Coated Brownies

Makes 16

These brownies are halfway between a biscuit and a cake, so the mixture does not rise a lot. However, if using an egg replacer, use 4 teaspoons of baking powder or the brownies may be a little heavy.

BROWNIES
125g/4oz/scant 1 cup dried dates
125g/4oz eating apple
180ml/6fl oz/scant ¾ cup water
60ml/2fl oz/¼ cup sunflower oil
2 large eggs
125g/4oz/¾ cup plus 2tbsp rice flour
60g/2oz/6tbsp carob flour
½tsp vanilla extract
2tsp baking powder

CAROB FROSTING
60g/2oz/scant ½ cup dried dates
30g/1oz/3tbsp carob flour
125ml/4fl oz/½ cup water
2tbsp light tahini
½tsp vanilla extract
toasted almonds, to decorate

1 To make the brownies, finely dice the dates and apple and simmer in the water until soft and reduced to a thick purée. Add a little more water if the mixture dries out before it is cooked.
2 Place the mixture in a food processor with the oil, eggs, flours, vanilla extract and baking powder. Process to mix. If you do not have a food processor, beat the eggs, then beat in the remaining ingredients, making sure the apple and dates are completely broken down.
3 Place in a greased and lined baking tray approximately 28 x 18 x 5cm/11 x 7 x ½ inches.
4 Bake in a preheated 200°C/400°F/gas mark 6 oven for 15–20 minutes or until risen and firm to the touch.
5 Allow to cool for 5 minutes in the baking tray, then turn out and remove the lining paper.

6 To make the frosting, finely dice the dates and simmer with the carob powder and water until smooth and thick. Remove from the heat. Add the tahini and vanilla extract and beat to combine. Allow to cool.
7 Cover the surface of the brownies with the frosting and sprinkle with toasted almonds. Cut into 16 pieces and serve.

Scotch Pancakes

Makes 12

These quick and easy pancakes are an ideal snack food when you feel like a tasty treat. They freeze well and can be toasted from frozen.

125g/4oz eating apple
60ml/2fl oz/¼ cup water
2 eggs
240ml/8fl oz/1 cup soya milk
125g/4oz/¾ cup plus 2tbsp potato flour
125g/4oz/¾ cup plus 2tbsp rice flour
2tsp baking powder
4tsp sunflower oil
½tsp lemon rind
oil for cooking

1. Stew the apple in the water until soft.
2. Place the apple, eggs, soya milk, flours, baking powder, sunflower oil and lemon rind in a food processor and process. If you do not have a processor, beat together by hand.
3. Place tablespoons of the mixture onto a greased griddle or frying pan and cook until bubbles rise to the surface and the underside is lightly browned. Turn over and cook the other side.
4. Serve warm with margarine and no-sugar jam or with stewed fruit and soya yogurt.

VARIATIONS

Cinnamon Scotch Pancakes

Replace the lemon rind with 1 teaspoon ground cinnamon in the above recipe.

Raisin Scotch Pancakes

Scatter a few raisins over the surface of each pancake once the mixture has been placed in the pan or griddle.

Cinnamon and Date Scones

Makes 8

The gram flour gives these scones an unusual nutty taste that goes well with the cinnamon and dates. The egg can be omitted if desired and replaced with an extra 60ml/2fl oz/¼ cup of milk and an extra teaspoon of baking powder.

- 125g/4oz/¾ cup plus 2tbsp rice flour
- 125g/4oz/¾ cup plus 2tbsp gram flour
- 1tsp ground cinnamon
- 60g/2oz/¼ cup margarine
- 1tbsp baking powder
- 60g/2oz/scant ½ cup chopped dates
- 1 egg
- 125ml/4fl oz/½ cup soya milk

1. Place the rice flour, gram flour, cinnamon, margarine and baking powder in a food processor and process. If you do not have a food processor, rub the margarine into the flours, cinnamon and baking powder.
2. Add the chopped dates, egg and sufficient soya milk to produce a very soft dough, when mixed. Do not over process or the dates will disintegrate.
3. Turn the mixture out on to a greased baking tray and shape into a round using a palette knife. Mark into 8 sections.
4. Bake in a preheated 200°C/400°F/gas mark 6 oven for approximately 15 minutes or until risen and beginning to brown.
5. Cool on a wire tray. Eat within 2 days or freeze.

Savoury Herb Scones

Makes 8

The gram flour in this recipe gives an unusual nutty flavour to these scones. They are delicious served with soup or salads, instead of bread. If desired, omit the egg and add an extra 60ml/2fl oz/¼ cup soya milk plus an extra teaspoon of baking powder.

125g/4oz/¾ cup plus 2tbsp rice flour
125g/4oz/¾ cup plus 2tbsp gram flour
60g/2oz/¼ cup margarine
1tbsp baking powder
1 heaped tsp dried basil
1tsp dried oregano
pinch salt and freshly ground black pepper
1tsp mustard
1 egg
125ml/4fl oz/½ cup soya milk
poppy seeds, to decorate

1 Place the rice flour, gram flour, margarine, baking powder, basil, oregano, salt, black pepper and mustard in a food processor and process. If you do not have a food processor, rub the margarine into the dry ingredients.
2 Add the egg and sufficient soya milk to make a very soft dough.
3 Turn the mixture out onto a greased baking tray and shape into a round using a palette knife. Mark into 8 sections. Sprinkle the surface with poppy seeds.
4 Bake in a preheated 200°C/400°F/gas mark 6 oven for approximately 15 minutes or until risen and beginning to brown
5 Cool on a wire tray. Eat within 2 days or freeze.

Rice Flour Bread

Bread is difficult to make without wheat flour, as it is the gluten in wheat which gives it its texture. This recipe, however, produces a loaf which has the texture of bread and a good flavour. The recipe is based on one given to me by a Philippine patient who adapted a traditional recipe. Vary the flavour by substituting herbs such as aniseeds, fennel seeds, caraway seeds, thyme, rosemary and marjoram.

150g/5oz/1 cup rice flour
225ml/8fl oz/1 cup soya milk
2 eggs
1tsp dried basil
1tsp dried oregano
¼tsp salt
2tsp baking powder

1. Soak the rice flour in the soya milk for at least 1 hour.
2. Separate the eggs and beat the egg whites in a large, clean bowl until very stiff.
3. Add the rice flour and milk to the egg whites along with the egg yolks, herbs, salt and baking powder. Gently mix, being careful not to beat out the air from the egg whites.
4. Place the mixture in a greased, 900g/2lb pudding basin (ovenproof bowl) and cover the bowl with a piece of greased foil, pleated in the middle to allow the loaf to expand. Tuck the foil well under the rim of the bowl and steam in a pressure cooker for 20 minutes or over a pan of boiling water for 1 hour 20 minutes.
5. Remove the foil and allow the loaf to cool for 10 minutes. Loosen the sides of the loaf with a knife, turn out on to a wire tray and allow to cool. Keep in an airtight container and eat within 3 days.

List of Suppliers

Gordon's Fine Foods
Gordon House, Littlemead, Cranleigh, Surrey, GU6 8ND.
Tel. 01483 267707 Fax. 01483 267783
Mail order suppliers of mustard flour with no other added ingredients and English mustard with salt, water and spices added.

Rio Trading Co (Health) Ltd
2 Centenary Estate, Hughes Rd, Brighton, East Sussex, BN2 4AW.
Tel. 01273 570987 Fax 01273 691226
Mail order suppliers of stevia herbal sugar alternative.

Hambleden Herbs
Court Farm, Milverton, Somerset, TA4 1NF.
Tel. 01823 401205 Fax. 01823 400276
Mail order suppliers of organic herbs and spices.

Neals Yard
29 John Dalton Street, Manchester, M2 6DS.
Tel. 0161 831 7875 Fax. 0161 835 9322
Mail order suppliers of herbs and spices.

Swinton Health Foods
177 Moorside Road, Swinton, Manchester, M27 9LD.
Tel. 0161 793 0091 Fax 0161 728 6087
Mail order suppliers of alternative and substitute foods, books and nutritional supplements.

Useful Addresses

SPNT (Society for the promotion of Nutritional Therapy)
PO Box 626, Woking, GU22 0XD.
Tel. 01483 740903
An educational and campaigning organisation with lay and practitioner members. Send SAE and £1 for information and a list of your nearest qualified nutritional therapists.

ION (The Institute of Optimum Nutrition)
Blades Court, Deodar Road, London, SW15 2NU
Tel. 0181 877 9993 Fax 0181 877 9980
ION exists as an independent charity to help you achieve optimum health. ION offers short courses, home study courses, books, a magazine, consultations and a Nutrition Consultants diploma course.

Higher Nature Ltd
Burwash Common, East Sussex, TN19 7LX
Tel. 01435 882880 Fax 01435 883720
Catologue of nutritional supplements and free magazine available on request. Also nutritional helpline for your queries, or nutrition consultations by phone, or in person.

The Nutritional Cancer Therapy Trust
Skyecroft, Wonham Way, Gomshall, Surrey, GU5 9NZ
Tel. 01483 202264 Fax. 01483 203130
A registered charity assisting in the application of natural therapies for the remission of cancer and other degenerative diseases.

York Nutritional Laboratory
Murton Way, Osbaldwick, York, Y19 5US
Tel. 01904 410410 Fax. 01904 422000
Provides 'pin prick' blood testing for allergies and food sensitivities to the general public, doctors and practitioners.

Allergy Care
1 Church Square,Taunton, Somerset, TA1 1SA
Tel. 01823 325023 Fax. 01823 325024
Mail order suppliers of some alternative and substitute food products. Also a team of qualified allergy testers (using vega testing) working in over 700 centres throughout the UK.

Alan Hopewell
South Gables, 2 Eleanor Rd, Bidston, Wirral, CH43 7QR
Tel. 0151 652 4277 Fax. 0161 652 5477
A bio-resonance practitioner who heads a group of holistic therapists throughout the United Kingdom who offer allergy testing (using vega testing) and nutritional advice.

Further Reading

Philosophy of Natural Therapeutics by Henry Lindlahr MD
CW Daniel Co. 1975. ISBN 0 85207 155 8

Passage to Power (natural menopause revolution) by Leslie Kenton
Vermilion. 1996. ISBN 00 09 180955 X

Why people don't heal and how they can by Caroline Myss PhD
Bantam. 1997. ISBN 0 553 50712 5

Hypoglycemia, a better approach by Dr Paavo Airola
Health Plus. 1997. ISBN 0 932090 01 X

Fats that Heal, Fats that Kill by Udo Erasmus
Alive Books. 1987. ISBN 0 920470 38 6

The Antibiotic Crisis by Leon Chaitow
Thorsons. 1998. ISBN 0 7225 3556 2

Healing with Whole Foods (oriental traditions and modern nutrition) by
Paul Pitchford
North Atlantic Books. 1993. ISBN 0 938190 64 4

Body Wisdom, Chinese and Natural Medicine for Self Healing by
Jennifer Harper
Thorsons. 1999. ISBN 0 7225 3368 3k

Bach flower therapy, The Complete approach by Mechthild Scheffer.
Thorsons. 1990. ISBN 0 7225 1121 3

Heal Thyself by Edward Back
The CW Daniel Co. 1995. ISBN 0 85207 301 1

The Healing power of Illness by Thorwald Dethlefsen
Element. 1999. ISBN 186 204 080 x

Encyclopedia of Natural Medicine by Michael Murray ND and Joseph Pizzorno ND
Little Brown and Company. 1998. ISBN 0 316 64678 4

Encyclopedia of Nutritional Supplements by Michael T. Murray ND
Prima Health. 1996. 0 7615 0410 9

Index